W9-BYH-976

THE BEST IN TENT CAMPING:

SOUTHERN CALIFORNIA

---

*A Guide for Car Campers Who Hate RVs, Concrete Slabs,
and Loud Portable Stereos*

Second Edition

THE BEST IN TENT CAMPING:

SOUTHERN CALIFORNIA

A Guide for Car Campers Who Hate RVs, Concrete Slabs, and Loud Portable Stereos

Second Edition

Bill Mai

Menasha
Ridge
Press, Inc.

Library of Congress Cataloging-in-Publication Data

Mai, Bill, 1945–
    The best in tent camping, southern California : a guide for campers who hate
RVs, concrete slabs, and loud portable stereos / Bill Mai.—2nd ed.
        p.   cm.
    Includes bibliographical references (p. 165)
    ISBN 0-89732-400-5
    1. Camping—California, Southern—Guidebooks.   2. Camp sites, facilities,
etc.—California, Southern—Guidebooks.   3. California—Guidebooks. I. Title.
GV191.42.C2 M25 2001
917.94'90454—dc21

                                                            2001034305

Cover design by Grant Tatum
Cover photo by Dennis Coello

Menasha Ridge Press
P.O. Box 43673
Birmingham, Alabama 35243
www.menasharidge.com

CONTENTS

The Northern Sierras

The Southern Sierras

Appendices

MAP LEGEND

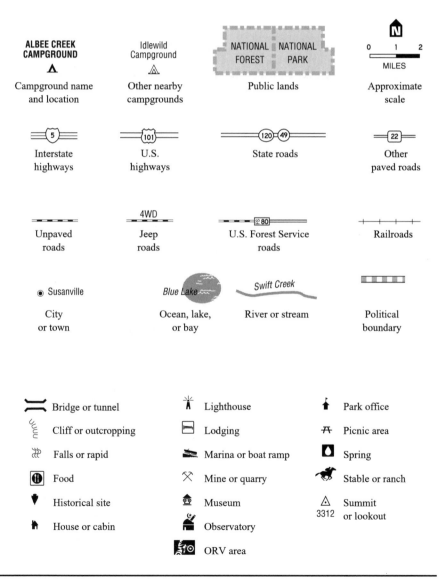

ALBEE CREEK CAMPGROUND

Campground name and location

Idlewild Campground

Other nearby campgrounds

NATIONAL FOREST   NATIONAL PARK

Public lands

0   1   2
MILES

Approximate scale

5

Interstate highways

101

U.S. highways

120 49

State roads

22

Other paved roads

Unpaved roads

4WD

Jeep roads

80

U.S. Forest Service roads

Railroads

● Susanville

City or town

Blue Lake

Ocean, lake, or bay

Swift Creek

River or stream

Political boundary

Bridge or tunnel

Cliff or outcropping

Falls or rapid

Food

Historical site

House or cabin

Lighthouse

Lodging

Marina or boat ramp

Mine or quarry

Museum

Observatory

ORV area

Park office

Picnic area

Spring

Stable or ranch

3312 Summit or lookout

Best in Tent Camping

CAMPGROUNDS

PREFACE

Friends and family get together, and pretty soon somebody starts talking about going camping, fishing the streams, and hiking the high country, and suddenly everybody wants to go. Usually the proposed trip fizzles out the next morning because nobody knows quite where to go, or how to arrange it, and nobody wants to end up camping in a little tent on a slab of concrete surrounded by hard-partying RVers. Nobody knows a sure good campground, so the whole camping adventure dies on the vine.

Well, that's why you buy this book. You'll discover almost 50 of the most wonderful spots to tent camp in Southern California and learn how to reserve a spot if necessary, what to expect, and how to get there. All the campgrounds will be beautiful, clean, safe, and well run.

The best are in the desert, along the coast, and in the mountains. Each of the campgrounds is rated in categories of beauty, site privacy, site spaciousness, quiet, security, and cleanliness/upkeep, so you pick the best from the best. There's not a loser here. Your choice will depend on what you like and what time of year you want to go camping.

I selected my campgrounds by going camping, by finding the tent-friendly campgrounds, by talking to rangers, and by buttonholing other campers or locals and asking them their favorite spot. I tried to be objective. I reined in my preference for big country pine and boulder-style campgrounds and gave the nod to some campgrounds located deep in the woods. I spaced out the campgrounds, I picked geographically as well as seasonally, and I stayed away from very small campgrounds because even if a few folks show up, they're full.

When you get out and start camping, you'll find your own hit parade of campgrounds. You'll stumble upon all the tiny gems with three or four sites and explore all the fantastic places in the mountains and desert where you can camp anywhere you want. It's a whole new world.

—*Bill Mai*

THE BEST IN TENT CAMPING:

SOUTHERN CALIFORNIA

A Guide for Car Campers Who Hate RVs, Concrete Slabs, and Loud Portable Stereos

Second Edition

INTRODUCTION

A Word about This Book and Southern California Camping

Drive from a campground below sea level in Death Valley to a campground 10,000 feet up by a glacier in the Sierras in two hours. This diversity is Southern California camping. The Big Sur coast is a wonder of the world. Anza-Borrego State Park is as big as Rhode Island. In the southern mountains, Mt. San Jacinto feels like little Switzerland. Near Julian, you'd swear you were in Vermont. This is a beautiful, beautiful area, and the tent camping is superb.

Geography

For the purposes of this book, Southern California is everything below a line drawn from Santa Cruz across the top of Yosemite National Park to the Nevada border. This area is divided into the Coast, the Desert, the Northern Sierras, and the Southern Sierras.

These four areas represent an amazing diversity in terrain. The Coast includes the 200 miles of sandy beaches north of the Mexican border to above Santa Barbara and the mountains that parallel the shore above the Los Angeles Basin to Santa Cruz. The Desert, in the southeast corner of California, is a vast and fascinating area of three deserts—Mojave, Colorado, and Sonoran—extending to the Colorado River. The Northern Sierras, or Sierra Nevada, the largest mountain mass in the United States, extends north from the Mojave Desert to Sequoia, Kings Canyon, and Yosemite. The Southern Sierras include the San Bernardinos and other minor ranges that extend southeast into Mexico.

Where to go and when

Pleasant camping can be found on the coast year-round. For winter and early spring camping head for the desert. Between Death Valley National Park, East Mojave National Preserve, Joshua Tree National Park, and Anza-Borrego Desert State Park you could camp all winter and never stay in the same spot twice. Camp the Northern and Southern Sierras in the spring, summer, and fall. Never camp the desert in the summer and only camp the mountains in the winter if you are prepared to go snow camping.

The rating system

The best campgrounds are rated in various categories—five stars is best, and one star is acceptable. Use the rating system to select the wonderful campground that combines the elements that best suit you.

Beauty

While all the campgrounds in this book are beautiful, some are absolutely sensational. They rate five stars. Mountains, streams, waterfalls, and sunsets all conspiring for a drop-dead campground personality. One- to four-star campgrounds are no dogs, either, but possess a less spectacular beauty that will grow on you.

Site privacy

Some campgrounds are beautifully built. The sites are arranged to take maximum advantage of the contour of the land, and the vegetation gives each one the most privacy possible. Good architecture cuts down on the cringe factor when other campers pull in next door. It makes you feel at home from the moment you step out of your car. What a difference!

Site spaciousness

I want flat land to pitch a tent on. And, I want the flat area far enough from the picnic table so my camping mate can make coffee without waking me and far enough away from the firepit so the embers don't burn little holes in the tent. And, I want a view. A view from each campsite is part of the spacious feeling that qualifies a campground for five stars in this category.

Quiet

Quiet is part of beautiful. There's nothing like the sound of a generator or a boom box to ruin a beautiful campsite. I consider white noise like the roar of a river to raise the quiet rating, since it is a natural noise and drowns out the sounds of other campers.

Security

Most of the campsites in this guide have campground hosts who keep a good eye on the property, which makes the campground safer than a good neighborhood. The farther the campground is from an urban center, the more secure it is. Of course, you can leave your valuables with the hosts if you're going to be gone for a day or so, but don't leave little things lying around. A blue jay will take off with a pair of sunglasses, and you never can tell what a visiting bear will decide has food value.

Cleanliness/Upkeep

Most campgrounds in this guide are well tended. Sometimes, on big weekends, places can get a little rank—not unlike one's kitchen after a big party. I appreciate the little things like the campground host who came around with a rake after each site was vacated to police the place. That particular campground received five stars in the cleanliness/upkeep department.

Good Planning

A little planning makes a good camping trip great. First, decide where and when you want to go. Then, phone that district's Ranger H.Q. to make sure the campground is open and that it has water. See if the ranger recommends other campgrounds. See if it's going to be busy. If it is, reserve ahead if possible. All National Forest campgrounds must be reserved at least ten days in advance. Remember, if you arrive and don't like the reserved site, the campground host will move you if another site is available.

Next, get your equipment together. Everybody knows what basics to bring tent camping. A tent (of course), the sleeping bags, a cooler, a stove, pots, utensils, a water jug, matches, a can opener, etc. But, it's those little things that you suddenly wish you had that make a happy camper. Number one objective is a good night's sleep.

Bring ear plugs. You need ear plugs to get a good snooze. The first night or two out camping, the unfamiliar flap of the tent drives you crazy if you

---

don't have ear plugs. Also, a snoring mate sleeping a foot away from you is nighttime hell on earth without ear plugs. In addition, ear plugs block out all that night nature stuff which interferes with a righteous camper's zzzzzs.

Don't forget to pack your own pillow. A good pillow gets your shoulders off the deck and lets your hips and behind take the weight. Use your clothes bag as an additional pillow (consider inflatable pillows sold at camping stores). Bring a thin foam mattress or buy the self-inflating pads. Buy a spidermat—a device that keeps your pad from slipping on the tent floor and keeps your sleeping bag on top of it. Air mattresses are okay, but susceptible to puncture. Never buy a double air mattress—every time your mate moves you get tossed around. Get a sleeping bag that is good and warm. Nothing is worse than being cold at night, and no sleeping bag is too warm. Just bring a sheet so you can sleep under it at first, then crawl into the bag when it gets nippy. Check the weather. If it's going to be cold, remember to bring socks and sweatpants to sleep in. A sweatshirt with a hood is invaluable, since you lose a lot of heat through your head.

Bring a water bottle to drink from at night. Consequently, a pee jar (a pee pot for ladies) just outside the tent is a great idea. You can stumble outside, use it, and empty it in the toilet in the morning.

Nothing disturbs your zzzzs like grit inside the tent, so bring something to put outside the tent to clean your feet on. In the woods, a square of AstroTurf works fine. At the seashore or in the desert, a tray full of water to dip your feet in works best. Bring a small brush for what grit leaks in.

Remember flashlights. The little mini-mags work okay, and if you take off the lens, you can hang them from a tent loop and actually read. Be careful since the little bulb is damn hot and will burn fabric or fingers. But, what works even better is a head lamp. You can buy them at any outdoor store. Just strap the lamp around your head with an adjustable elastic band. Everywhere you look, there's light. They're great for finding stuff, cleaning up in the dark after dinner, and reading. Remember duct tape. "If you can't fix it, duct tape it" is a camping maxim.

Bring a sponge to clean off the picnic table. A plastic tablecloth is nice, too (bring little pushpins to secure it so it won't blow away). A plastic bowl or a blow-up sink from Basic Designs (around $6 at Sports Mart) is invaluable for washing dishes. Picnic table benches get mighty hard, so bring a cushion. Buy a cheap lawn chair, and get the inexpensive umbrella that attaches to the back of the chair, so you can sit around camp out of the sun. While sitting around, you'll want a fly swatter to wreak revenge on a lazy droning fly or two and mosquito repellent for that irksome gnat in your ear. Bring a little leaf rake to police your camp area. Remember binoculars, a bird book, and a wildflower book, so you can put a name with what you see.

Good water jugs are two-and-a-half gallon plastic jobs sold in supermarkets. On most of them, you can twist the top off and refill them. They travel best with their valves up to avoid any leakage. Take a hot shower. Basic Designs (and other outfits) sells a solar shower bag that really works. After a day in the sun sitting on a hot rock, the water is hot! Or, bring along nonscented diaper wipes for a quick sponge bath. They work.

Don't be afraid to ask fellow campers for help or for stuff you might have forgotten. All campers know what it's like to forget basic stuff and love to help fellow campers. There's always a mechanic on vacation camping next site over when your car won't start or somebody with extra white gas for your stove. Think hearty about your fellow campers. Wave and say, "Hi."

The campfire is an important camp event. Stores around the campground sell bundles of wood, and often, the campground host and hostess sell wood. Also, there may be windfalls around the campground from which you can take wood (ask the campground host). You need a good camp saw for that. An absolute essential is a can of charcoal starter fluid. This guarantees a fire even in a driving rain. Naturally, don't forget marshmallows, graham crackers, and chocolate for roasting.

Fix your car up before you go. Nothing can be a bigger bummer than a mechanical breakdown on your way. Have a mechanic check your water hoses and the air pressure in your tires before you load up. Remember, your car will be loaded down with stuff, and this will put a strain on your tires and cooling system. Bring an extra fan belt. Nothing can shut down the car like a snapped fan belt that you have to special order from Japan. Even if you don't know a fan belt from third base, bring one. Somebody will come along who knows how to install it. Make sure your spare tire is correctly inflated. Mishap #999 is when you put on your spare, let the car down, and find out the spare is flat.

If you fish, be sure to get a license and display it. Fishing without a license is a misdeamenor, punishable by a maximum fine of $1000 and/or six months in jail. On your way into the campground, stop at a local store and find out what the folks are using for bait. Buy it. This will save you a lot of experimentation and probably provide you with a good meal.

Remember the bears! We have few mosquitoes here in Southern California, but a lot of black bears. Never leave your cooler out. Put it in the trunk or disguise it with a blanket if you have a hatchback or a van. Don't eat in your tent. Take all cosmetics, soap, etc. and put them in the car. Disguise them, too. A bear will rip off a car door to get a tube of chapstick. Bring a small bottle of Clorox to wipe down your picnic table at night. Bears don't like Clorox (but, don't put too much faith in this!). If a bear raids your camp looking for food, shoo him away like you would a naughty dog. Don't worry. Even the boldest bears don't go into tents unless they smell food.

Think about dispersed camping. With a fire permit, a shovel, and a bucket of water, you can camp just about anywhere in the National Forests (consult Ranger District H.Q.), and, of course, in Anza-Borrego Desert State Park. The fire permit costs nothing, and there are miles and miles of fire roads and lumber roads you can explore to find the dispersed campground of your dreams.

Settling in

When you come into a campground be aware of a certain psychological barrier. This is a new place. Suddenly, you've driven all this way, and the campground doesn't look that hot. You feel disappointed. You feel like the "new kid at school." The other campers look up from their game of gin rummy and hope you won't camp next to them as you drive around the campground loops and look helplessly at the open sites. Nothing looks good enough.

Park your car. Pull into the first available site that could possibly do. Then, walk around the campground. You have half an hour to decide before you pick your site and pay. Once you get out and walk, you'll break through that "new kid at school" dilemma and soon feel like you're a part of the place. It's odd. Suddenly, you don't mind camping next to the gin rummy players. You realize that this is your campground as well as theirs. By the next morning, the whole place will feel like home, and the gin rummy players will seem like the best of neighbors. You won't understand why you didn't immediately recognize this campground as the best of all campgrounds.

When you plan a camping trip, try to stay in one campground for at least three days. Stay one day, and you end up spending most of your time packing and unpacking and getting familiar with the campground. Stay three days and you'll relax and have fun.

Go tent camping. Live in paradise for a few days. Camping makes you want to sin like the damned, sleep like the righteous, and hike like the last of the great American walkers. Balm for the weary soul!

SOUTHERN CALIFORNIA

THE COAST

ANDREW MOLERA STATE PARK

Big Sur

Go to Andrew Molera State Park and walk the 1-mile trail to the ocean. The beach is awesome—4 miles of Big Sur's longest beach. Find sea fig, sand verbena, silverwood, and beach primrose on the side of the dunes. On the bluffs, look for seaside painted cups, sea lettuce, beach sagewort, and coast eriogonum. On my last trip to Andrew Molera, I brought a plant identification book and actually identified a few of the species named above.

I had better luck with the birds. I saw black long-necked cormorants off Molera Point, willits, and a great blue heron. Look for the mass of tiny sanderlings that flow in behind the waves to feed before the breakers come again. They are looking for small sand crabs.

When I visited Andrew Molera in March, I hiked out on the Headlands Trail and saw a pod of gray whales heading south. Also, keep an eye out for otters. They are actually members of the weasel family with slim bodies, high hips, broad heads, and short furry tails. Weighing in at about 80 pounds, the otter has feet that function like hands, so they can use rocks as hammers to smash shells. They have lovely, light whiskers and live together, in groups called rafts, in the kelp beds a mile or so from shore. This is where the mothers teach their babies to swim down and get food from the ocean floor below. They also teach them to hide

CAMPGROUND RATINGS

Beauty: ★★★★★
Site privacy: ★★★★
Site spaciousness: ★★★★
Quiet: ★★★★
Security: ★★★★
Cleanliness/upkeep: ★★★★

Andrew Molera has it all— Big Sur, a river, the sea, mountains full of big trees, and tent camping in a grassy meadow.

among the bulbs of the bull kelp, so the great white shark can't find them and eat them.

Once thought extinct, the otters are still an endangered species. The last count was 2,239 otters (including pups) living along the California coast—ranging from Vandenberg Air Force Base in Santa Barbara County to the San Francisco Bay.

Storms that separate pups from their mothers are a big problem, since pups can't survive alone. The lucky ones are washed ashore and found by nice folks, who

take them to the Monterey Bay Aquarium for rehabilitation. Here, they are paired with a surrogate mother and are taught to swim, hunt food, and groom their fur. The surrogates are not other otters, but scientists in diving gear!

From the bluffs, the ocean reflects incredible colors. The purer the water, the deeper the color—this prismatic show all depends on how the sunlight is scattered by the water molecules. The old lava beds of Point Sur show the rainbow shades, and the kelp beds turn spots of blue to deep green. The light blue and turquoise along the cliffs are caused by the surf forcing air into the water. Plumes of red, brown, and green are the streams pouring Santa Lucia silt into the ocean.

The camping in Andrew Molera is pure tent camping. The sites are in a beautiful, grassy meadow a short walk from the parking lot (the last time I was there I had a cooler heavy with ice, beer, and soda and wished I'd brought one of those airport dollies you use to carry heavy suitcases). There are vault toilets and piped water spigots set around the meadow. The campsites are not numbered, and the Ranger told me there is no limit to the camping capacity. The crowd was young and very friendly. And the price ($3) is right as rain. There is a three-day limit, and then you have to stay away for seven days before returning.

The Big Sur River meanders through Andrew Molera offering good sandy banks for sunbathing and shallow water for wading. But the ocean here is rough, cold, and often windy. Only the make-shift huts built by sunbathers let you brave the afternoon wind. Beware of rogue waves, and don't get blocked by the tides.

There is no excuse for not having a campfire at Andrew Molera. You are permitted to collect up to 50 pounds of driftwood from the beach. All other wood in the park is protected. Really lazy people can purchase firewood at the stores along CA 1.

You'll find good hiking east of the highway. As you climb the East Molera Trail, see madrone, coast live oak, canyon oak, and then redwood at the crest of the ridge. Look for Indian paintbrush, red elderberry, and red maids. Keep going when the trail ends and reach the South Fork Little Sur River down the other side of the ridge.

KEY INFORMATION

Andrew Molera State Park
c/o Pfeiffer Big Sur State Park #1
Big Sur, CA 93920

Operated by: California Department of Parks and Recreation

Information: (831) 667-2315; http://parks.ca.gov

Open: All year

Individual sites: Unnumbered/no limit

Each site has: Limited picnic tables, fireplaces

Registration: Self registration; ranger will come collect fee

Facilities: Water, vault toilets

Parking: In parking lot; walk to campground

Fee: $3 ($2 per person per day use fee plus $1 per person overnight fee)

Elevation: Near sea level

Restrictions:

Pets—On 6-foot or shorter leash only

Fires—In fireplaces

Vehicles—Not allowed in campgrounds

Other—3-day stay limit (must vacate for 7 days to return)

To get there: from San Francisco, drive south on CA 1 to Carmel, then drive 21 miles south on CA 1 to Andrew Molera State Park on the right.

FREMONT PEAK STATE PARK

San Juan Bautista

Fremont Peak State Park is deliriously beautiful in April and May, when the spring grasses are green and feathery, and the flowers are blooming. It's a great place to go when the coast is socked in with fog. Climb to the peak and look out over the richest farmland and the richest marine area in the world.

The drive up to the park from San Juan Bautista is alternately lovely, chilling, and lovely again. At first, you take a winding, old country road out of the valley and up into oaks draped with mistletoe. Then you burst into *Road Warrior* country. On the left is the Hollister Hills State Vehicular Recreation Area, where off-road enthusiasts bring their vehicles. It's a land of tire-ripped hills and torched brush. Scary. But persevere and you arrive at the mountain-top to enter Fremont Peak State Park with its oaks, pines, and incredible views.

The camping here is primitive and best suited for tents. All the sites are roomy, grassy, and shaded by oaks. There is potable water, and each site boasts an incredible view of Monterey Bay. However, it is best to avoid the area in the summer, when Gavilan Peak is overrun by nasty, little biting flies.

Fremont Peak State Park is actually *not* situated on Fremont Peak, but on Gavilan Peak. The expansive view from Gavilan prompted John C. Fremont to build a fort there one fateful day in 1846. California,

CAMPGROUND RATINGS

Beauty:	★★★★★
Site privacy:	★★★
Site spaciousness:	★★★★
Quiet:	★★★★
Security:	★★★
Cleanliness/upkeep:	★★★

Come to Fremont Peak State Park for spring camping and to San Juan Bautista for California's yesterdays. You won't regret it.

then a territory of Mexico, was seething. The Mexican government wanted to get rid of the American settlers, who were forming ragtag armies to take the territory. In additon, Native Americans were arming and trying to retake their former lands. Into the middle of this rode John C. Fremont, a Captain of the Topographical Engineers of the United States, to map the California Trail.

Jose Castro, the Mexican governor, ordered Fremont and his group of Delaware Native Americans and hard-bitten frontiersman to leave the territory. Fremont refused. Cheekily, he marched his men up Gavilan Peak and built a rough log fort within plain sight of General Castro's headquarters in San Juan Bautista. Fremont raised the American flag up a stripped sapling. His men cheered, but general Castro was livid. He posted a proclamation: "Fellow Citizens: A band of robbers commanded by a captain of the United States Army, J. C. Fremont, have without respect to the laws and authorities of the department, daringly introduced themselves into the country and disobeyed the orders both of your commander-in-chief and of the prefect of the district." Castro summoned a band of Mexican cavalrymen from Monterey north to San Juan.

Fremont set an ambush for the cavalrymen, but at the last minute, the Mexican officers inexplicably ordered their troops back to Monterey. Meanwhile, on the peak, the westerly wind kicked up and blew the crude flagpole down. Taking this as a sign, Fremont abandoned his fort and grudgingly retreated.

General Castro called the Americans "cowards and poor guests," and the incident was over, but both Fremont and Castro would play giant roles in the subsequent turn over of Mexican California to the United States.

Near the campground is the Fremont Park Observatory, with a 30-inch reflecting telescope. They have special programs in the spring and fall. Write The Fremont Park Observatory Association, P.O. Box 787, San Juan Bautista, CA 95045, or phone (831) 623-2465, for a schedule.

A good hike to the peak begins in the parking lot. You'll see a road and a trail. The trail, signed with a hiker's symbol, leads to the observatory. Take the road for a short distance, then join the signed Peak Trail, which circles the mountain.

On the high ridges, see Coulter pine and madrone. The northern slopes are full of manzanita, toyon, and scrub oak, and the southern slopes spill over with grasses and wildflowers. Don't forget your binoculars.

Visit San Juan Bautista, once the district headquarters of the northern half of Alta, California. The 1906 earthquake destroyed half the town, and soon cows grazed on the Plaza. As Will Durant once said, "Civilization exists by geological consent, subject to change without notice." San Juan slept until it was resurrected by benefactors of the old mission and the California Department of Parks and Recreation. I can't count the number of times I have driven U.S. 101 and passed by San Juan Bautista. However, after one visit, I'm a believer. The Old Mission and the Plaza have been lovingly restored.

KEY INFORMATION

Fremont Peak State Park
P.O. Box 1110
San Juan Bautista, CA 95045

Operated by: California Department of Parks and Recreation

Information: (831) 623-4255 or (831) 623-4881; http://parks.ca.gov; at the San Juan Bautista State Historic Park

Open: All year (avoid summer)

Individual sites: 25

Each site has: Picnic table, fire ring

Registration: At entrance

Facilities: Water, pit toilets

Parking: At site

Fee: $7, $5 per extra vehicle

Elevation: 2,750 feet

Restrictions:

Pets—Allowed; $1 per dog

Fires—In fire rings (no firewood available at campgrounds)

Vehicles—18-foot trailers, 26-foot RVs

Other—$1 day use fee

To get there: from L.A., drive 330 miles north on U.S. 101 to Salinas, then continue north on U.S. 101 a few miles and turn east on CA 156. Turn right (south) on San Juan Canyon Road and drive 11 miles to the campground along a narrow, winding road.

THE COAST

KIRK CREEK CAMPGROUND /
PLASKETT CREEK CAMPGROUND

Lucia, Los Padres National Forest

Kirk Creek and Plaskett Creek campgrounds are like fraternal twins. They occupy the most isolated stretch of CA 1, north of San Simeon and south of Big Sur. About 5 miles apart, on the best stretch of Los Padres National Forest coastline, these campgrounds offer the most relaxed camping on the entire Southern California coast.

Kirk Creek lies on a bluff overlooking the ocean. Set in gorse, it gets quite a lot of wind. Of course, the view is shockingly immediate—as if you are suspended over the ocean itself. The sites are separated and private until you stand up; the brush surrounding the sites is about chest high. This does give you some relief from the oceanic blasts. Thankfully, there's a fence along the edge of the precipice. However, just south, there are goat trails leading down to a rocky point and a sandy cove at low tide. Navigate these trails during the daylight hours.

Plaskett Creek Campground is oriented more toward small RVs, with larger and more level sites. Plaskett is farther from the beach, behind a line of Monterey pines, and not as subject to the ocean's gusty blasts. The area is nice and grassy. The sites are roomier, but not as private—without the impenetrable gorse cover of Kirk.

I love both campgrounds. Many CA 1 tourists speed through this area, because you feel as if you're between the devil and the deep blue sea here.

CAMPGROUND RATINGS

Beauty: ★★★★★
Site privacy: ★★★★★
Site spaciousness: ★★★★★
Quiet: ★★★★★
Security: ★★★
Cleanliness/upkeep: ★★★★★

Come for the huge cliffs of jade. Stay for great camping and hiking in the mountains.

The nearby U.S. Forest Service station at Pacific Valley is primarily used as a fire station. An area map and other information are posted outside the station. The station does not have regularly scheduled hours of operation, but when personnel are on duty they are available to assist visitors. Maps are for sale.

There is mountain hiking in the mountains directly east of the campground. Though the hiking is good and the weather is cool, the big draw here is the beach. Go to aptly named Jade Cove to see the huge cliffs made entirely of jade. What a magical experience! Walk down from the picnic area, over the cattle gate to the beach, and, as the stairs hit the sand, you'll see the jade on the left. Then, continue south on the beach. I came here once as a child and was overwhelmed by the magic of the green rock, the huge whips of kelp, the surf and white spume, and the shockingly cold water.

Child or adult, no one can help but react viscerally to the primordial beauty of this coastline. We are all drawn to the sea. Why? Our bodies are mostly water, and our blood has the same saline content as the sea. We are carried in water in the womb. Another explanation reaches farther back than that, to a dark age of humanity, known as the Pliocene Gap, from four to seven million years ago. Herbivorous apes went into it, and carnivorous ape-men came out of it. There are no fossils to explain the transformation, but one au courant theory holds that our ancestors passed through a water-living stage.

This would explain the layer of subcutaneous fat unique to humans, as well as the partial webbing between our fingers and toes. Our spines are more flexible than apes, allowing us to swim, and we have a sense of balance equal to sea lions. We are streamlined (having very little hair) and can hold our breath for as long as three-and-a-half minutes. Humans also possess a diving reflex, like other marine animals that closes down our airways and slows our heart to half speed. Human babies, unlike apes, automatically hold their breath under water.

Theorists believe that the sea-ape got a taste for fish and shellfish and returned to land with an expanded taste for meat

For another ocean experience, go pebble hunting on the San Simeon coast. Find jadite and brown and green chert pebbles. Native Americans fashioned arrowheads from chert. The best hunting is on Moonstone Beach. Turn off CA 1 in Cambria at Windsor Boulevard, then go northwest about 0.4 mile on Moonstone Beach Drive to the state beach parking area. Go down to the beach and walk northwest to the cliff. Also, try the beach at Pico Creek, 2.5 miles north of San Simeon Beach Campground.

In July and August, be sure to get to Kirk or Plaskett by Thursday. They fill up, and no reservations are accepted for groups of less than 25. Tent campers should stop at the Ranger Station between the two campgrounds and get directions to dispersed camping areas in the nearby wilderness.

To get there: from San Francisco, drive south on CA 1 through Monterey to Lucia. Then drive 4 miles farther south on CA 1 to Kirk Creek Campground on the right. Plaskett Creek Campground is 5.5 miles still farther south from Kirk Creek Campground. After you pass the Ranger Station, Plaskett Creek will be on your left.

KEY INFORMATION

Kirk Creek Campground / Plaskett Creek Campground
Los Padres National Forest
6144 Calle Real
Goleta, CA 93117

Operated by: U.S. Forest Service

Information: (805) 683-6711 or (831) 385-5434; www.r5.fs.fed.us/lospadres

Open: All year

Individual sites: Kirk 33; Plaskett 44

Each site has: Picnic table, fireplace

Registration: At entrance

Facilities: Water, flush toilets

Parking: At site

Fee: $16

Elevation: Near sea level

Restrictions:
Pets—On leash only
Fires—In fireplaces
Vehicles—Small RVs

THE COAST

LION CAMPGROUND

Rose Valley, Los Padres National Forest

Lion Campground is the nearest get-away-from-it-all destination to Los Angeles. Other campgrounds closer to L.A. are only islands in the urban sea, while Lion Campground is on the edge of the wilderness. And, it is only a quick hour and a half from Santa Monica.

This entire area was once grizzly country. Jeff Howard, one of the area's first Anglo residents, loved to hunt grizzly. He said he could always scare one up on short notice. However, the history of the poor grizzly bear (Ursus arctos) in California is a disasterous story. California is the only state in the union that has an extinct animal as its symbol. The last grizzly in Southern California was killed in Trabuco Canyon in 1908. The last one in the state was killed in 1922. Old grizzly weighed about 900 pounds and used his long claws and muscle to rip up roots, bulbs, and tubers, as well as to tear up logs to get ants and termites. He roamed the lowlands and the valleys, and that's where he ran into the aforementioned Jeff Howard.

Howard was also famous for killing a Basque sheepherder in a gunfight in 1877. Locked in the Ventura jail, he promptly escaped and rode back to his place near Lion Campground to hunt more grizzly. The good townspeople were outraged, so Howard lit out for Arizona. The sheriff put a $500 reward on his head, and Howard was arrested in Prescott, Arizona, and

CAMPGROUND RATINGS

Beauty: ★★★★
Site privacy: ★★
Site spaciousness: ★★★
Quiet: ★★★
Security: ★★
Cleanliness/upkeep: ★★

Lion Campground offers good stream swimming, trout fishing, and hiking in the Sespe wilderness.

returned to jail in Ventura. This time, he filed through his leg irons, tore open the window bars of the new town jail, and escaped.

Howard's pal, the editor of the local newspaper, would report on his health from time to time, which infuriated the locals, but Howard was gone, never to be seen again. Reportedly, he died in bed in 1910 somewhere in Arizona.

Tucked into narrow Lion's Canyon, Lion Campground is squeezed alongside high, rounded hills by a branch of the Sespe Creek. The swimming hole near the middle of the camp is a good one. The water feels like silk, and schools of trout nose upstream waiting for something delectable to float by. Lion's Canyon drops off into some wild country, so the hiking is superb.

There's a Shangri-la atmosphere about the place. Up high enough, Lion's Canyon and the nearby Rose Valley often escape the spring fog blahs that blanket the coast. I think spring and fall are the prime times to visit; it's too hot in the summer for me. Most of the other campers are hikers or hiking fishermen, and those folks usually go to sleep early, which makes for a quiet campground. Lion Campground has piped water, but system problems cause it to be shut off occasionally—so bring water. The campsites have very little cover—again favoring a fall or spring rather than a summertime visit when it gets crowded.

Classic Lower Chaparral, Lion's Canyon has greasewood and ceanothus growing on the south-facing slopes. Greasewood is a shrub standing anywhere from two to fifteen feet high with small needle-like leaves. Its flowers are small, white, and grow in showy clusters. California lilacs (or ceanothus) have a smooth, olive green bark. Rub the pale blue flowers for a moment or two in water, and they will develop a cleansing lather. That's why this plant is sometimes called "soap bush."

On the north-facing slopes, find scrub oaks, coffeeberry, and holly-leaved cherry. Scrub oaks are hard to miss, because of their evergreen leaves and acorn fruit. Holly-leaved cherry is an evergreen shrub with white flowers that forms a purple-black fruit. Bees like it, and Native Americans fermented the fruits into an intoxicating drink. Coffeeberry is another shrub with small greenish flowers that forms a soft green, black, or red fruit shaped like a commercial coffee bean. Native Americans used the berries to correct the effects of an acorn diet, and the bark was used as a laxative. In the vine department, look for wild peas, honeysuckle, and wild cucumbers.

A couple miles away (you would have passed the turnoff on your way in) is the Rose Valley Falls Campground. The falls is a scenic highlight in this section of Los Padres National Forest—especially in the winter and spring when there is enough water in Rose Valley Creek to make a splash. It's only a short hike from the campground to the falls, and a trail continues around to the top of the falls.

A good night walk is back up the road from Lion Campground. You can't get lost, and the view is spectacular.

If you want to camp this area when Lion Campground is closed, go a few miles south to Wheeler Gorge Campground. You'll find reservable family camping with some decent trout fishing thrown in.

KEY INFORMATION

Lion Campground
Los Padres National Forest
6144 Calle Real
Goleta, CA 93117

Operated by: U.S. Forest Service

Information: (805) 640-9060; www.r5.fs.fed.us/lospadres

Open: April to December

Individual sites: 30

Each site has: Picnic tables, fireplaces

Registration: At entrance

Facilities: Vault toilets, water (call ahead to confirm)

Parking: At site

Fee: $7

Elevation: 3,000 feet

Restrictions:

Pets—On leash only

Fires—In fireplaces

Vehicles—RVs and trailers under 16 feet

Other—Lion Campground is closed periodically to protect the habitats and populations of threatened and endangered species. Sometimes, would be campers may hike in and camp in designated areas only. Always call ahead when planning a trip to Lion Campground.

To get there: from L.A., drive west on U.S. 101 to CA 33. Go north to Ojai. From Ojai, drive 15 miles north on CA 33. Turn right (east) onto Sespe River Road and drive 7 miles to the campground.

MALIBU CREEK STATE PARK

Malibu

Situated on a big hunk of the most coveted real estate in Southern California and surrounded by the rapidly encroaching megalopolis of the L.A. area, Malibu Creek State Park Campground is a precious gem. It is beautiful! With sections once owned by Bob Hope, Ronald Reagan, and 20th Century-Fox, the park now covers over 7,000 acres. This is a great place to tent camp in fall, winter, and spring. Protected by a mountain range from the springtime fog blahs that hit the beaches in Southern California, Malibu Creek State Park is situated between two major tourist thoroughfares—CA 1 and U.S. 101. It's just 40 miles down the hill to Malibu and all the wonderful beaches. You're also near Santa Barbara on U.S. 101 and Universal City to the east.

You'll find safe mountain biking and hiking, so this is a great place to bring children camping. It's also a good first night's camp if you are flying into LAX and a good escape from L.A. if you happen to live there. I've camped at Malibu Creek State Park several times over Saturday night with my wife, eaten at the nearby Saddle Peak Lodge (excellent food), then ducked back to our humble tent for a weekend combining the high life and the great outdoors.

High season at the campground begins with spring break and goes through the end of September. Since Malibu Creek is

CAMPGROUND RATINGS

Beauty: ★★★★★
Site privacy: ★
Site spaciousness: ★★
Quiet: ★★★
Security: ★★★★★
Cleanliness/upkeep: ★★★★

Malibu Creek State Park is a good base camp from which to explore Los Angeles. It's also good for kids with its easy hiking and bicycling.

a first come, first served campground, be sure to come early on weekends during the summer. The ranger recommended arriving by noon on Friday to reserve a spot for a summer weekend. The campground is very clean, well patrolled, and well maintained, but the sites themselves are unremarkable. The incredible vista and the "neighborhood" are what make this a fun camping experience.

A good introductory walk is along Shady Trail to Century Lake, then back again. From the camground, walk down to a wide fire road. Cross the stream, and you'll see that the road splits into a high road and a low road. Either one will do. Pass the Visitor Center and find the Gorge Trail. Follow it upstream to where the creek turns dramatically around volcanic rock cliffs into the Rock Pool. Remember the *Tarzan* movies and the "Swiss Family Robinson" TV series? Parts from both were filmed here.

Back on the high road, you'll come to the crest of a hill where you can look down on Century Lake. Look around carefully and spot the distinctive hills that doubled for Korean terrain in the television series "M*A*S*H." When I first hiked the park, part of the set was still lying around, and you could feel the ghosts of Hawkeye, Radar, and all those choppers.

A challenging hike is up to the Backbone Trail. From there, you could conceivably hike all the way to Will Rogers State Park in Los Angeles. Don't try it, though, unless you are a walking fool. Farther on is a swampy pond always good for bird-watching, and then Ronald Reagan's ranch with some good hiking. (Obtain a good map of the park from the ranger at the gate for $1.)

Note that wood fires are only allowed from December to May because of summer fire hazards. This area is near the scene of the 1996 fire that burned down into the heart of Malibu Canyon, wreaking havoc on forests and homes. Fires in the Lower Chaparral are as common as cats and so much a part of the cycle of nature that Native Americans would set controlled fires to help Mother Nature along. They were interested in burning the brush fuel underneath the bigger trees that they used for food before the brush grew enough to burn the larger trees. Fire, also, allowed more access and helped expose the game animals.

My favorite time of year here is fall to spring—their off season. I find the mountains too hot in the summer for hiking or biking (pack a canteen if you decide to visit then). However, camping at Malibu Creek State Park in the summer would afford one a good base camp to hit the beach and other L.A. summer tourist attractions. Note that the Renaissance Fair is held just up the road at the Paramount Ranch (in Santa Monica Mountains National Recreation Area) along with an old-time western town used in several movies.

KEY INFORMATION

Malibu Creek State Park
Angeles District, Malibu Sector
1925 Las Virgenes Road
Calabasas, CA 91302

Operated by: California Department of Parks and Recreation

Information: (818) 880-0350; http://parks.ca.gov

Open: All year

Individual sites: 45 tent sites; 4 RV sites

Each site has: Picnic table, fire pits, no hookups

Registration: By park entrance; reserve by phone, (800) 444-7275, or online, www.reserveamerica.com

Facilities: Water, flush toilets, hot solar showers (all accessible to disabled patrons)

Parking: By site

Fee: $14–19; $8.65 nonrefundable reservation fee

Elevation: 500 feet

Restrictions:

Pets—On leash only; in campground only

Fires—In fire pits only

Vehicles—RV maximum length 32 feet

Other—Be careful with fire

To get there: from Santa Monica, drive north up CA 1 through Malibu, turn right on Malibu Canyon Road and drive 6 miles to the park entrance on the left. From the San Fernando Valley, drive north on U.S. 101 to the Las Virgenes exit and drive 4 miles southwest on Las Virgenes Road to the park entrance.

COAST

MANRESA UPLANDS STATE BEACH

La Selva Beach

Manresa Uplands State Beach offers the best in beach tent camping in Southern California. In fact, RVs are not even allowed. Cars must be parked in a designated lot a few hundred yards away from the sites. It's wonderful. There's a 20-minute parking area near the campsites where you can unload your equipment, carry it to your campsite, and then move your car to the lot. In a land where RV campers outnumber tent campers three to one, this is tenting bliss.

The campground lies on a bluff overlooking Monterey Bay. Eucalyptus and Monterey pine shade the well-spaced sites. A trail leads down to an endless sandy beach, good for swimming, sunbathing, and walking. This is a popular campground, as well it should be. Reserve early and plan on spending some time here. It wouldn't be a bad idea to buy one of those big two-room tents, which go on sale in early summer ($200 maximum). You want inside space to stand up and move around and aluminum chairs for sitting around. Think Victorian-style summer camping—luxury equipment and comforts such as thick summer novels.

Look out over Monterey Bay and imagine the wilderness below inhabited by kingdoms of marine creatures. Under the surface of the bay are forests of giant kelp. The kelp's tough stems, or stipes, climb more than 100 feet from the ocean floor,

CAMPGROUND RATINGS

Beauty:	★★★★★
Site privacy:	★★★
Site spaciousness:	★★★★
Quiet:	★★★★
Security:	★★★★
Cleanliness/upkeep:	★★★★★

Manresa Uplands State Beach offers the best tent camping on the Southern California beach. Think Victorian-style camping, bring equipment, and reserve ahead.

supporting the plant's flat, golden-brown fronds, which are held afloat by small, gas-filled bulbs. In late summer or early winter, look for bull kelp piled up on the shore. You'll recognize it by the air bladders at the base of each blade. (Native Americans ate the bull kelp and made musical instruments from the hollow stipes and bladders—a section of stipe and half a bladder can make a trumpet!) The bull kelp rots on shore and shelters millions of sand hoppers that become breakfast, lunch, or dinner for the sandpipers.

Half a mile off the beach, a large submarine canyon slashes across the sea bed. It's big enough for the Grand Canyon to fit inside easily. There are reefs, rocks, and underwater granite, volcanic cliffs that mirror the canyonlands in the Southwest. Rich nutrients, accumulated for centuries, are caught in the upwelling of deep ocean waters and thrown up toward the surface to support a marine community so rich that it contains every marine habitat known to man except coral reefs and mangrove swamps. The submerged rocks are carpeted with sponges and sea anemones. The rainbow of underwater Monterey Bay comprises reds, pinks, blues, and purples. A ceiling of kelp leaves covers the ocean's surface, allowing beams of sunlight to highlight the amber leaves. Some say it's like a magnificent cathedral with stained glass windows.

Go to Monterey for scuba lessons—Monterey Bay is a mecca for scuba divers from around the world. The first divers here were Native Americans called *Ohlone* (abalone people) who shared the shellfish with the sea otter. Then came the Japanese who dove for abalone and lined the sandy Monterey roads with great piles of discarded red abalone shells. When Jacques Cousteau invented scuba (self-contained underwater breathing apparatus) gear during World War II, the abalone were already thinning out, and the industry cried out even then for strict regulation.

According to an anonymous traveler in 1850, the road from Monterey north to the campground was "a mere trail through thick chaparral, crossing some deep ravines...with grizzlies living in the brush, particularly bold and savage." Most people traveled by boat. The Pajaro Valley, away from the sand dunes, was rich, marshy land—more like a lake in winter. It was full of birds. They say you could clap your hands, wait a three-count, fire your shotgun up into the air, and kill a hundred birds without aiming. Today, this is some of the richest and most heavily chemically treated farmland in the world. Note the fields behind the campground stubbornly holding out against creeping urban development.

Look at the artichoke fields, and imagine the city of brown meadow mice living in them (about 3,000 mice per acre). They eat the artichoke leaves and stems while dodging hawks, owls, crows, and gulls. I've read that gulls hate crows so bad that they will attack a lucky crow with a captured mouse just to make him drop it—out of pure spite and malice.

Visit Santa Cruz. Downtown is very charming. Pedestrian friendly, it has bookstores, sidewalk restaurants, brew pubs, surfer museums, outdoor markets, and a horde of handsome students from the university on the hill. Very user-friendly, Santa Cruz wants your tourist dollar and gives you good value for it.

KEY INFORMATION

Manresa Uplands State Beach Campground
205 Manresa Beach Road
La Selva Beach, CA 95076

Operated by: California Department of Parks and Recreation

Information: (831) 761-1795; http://parks.ca.gov

Open: Mid-March to October

Individual sites: 64

Each site has: Picnic table, fire ring

Registration: At entrance; reserve by phone, (800) 444-7275, or online, www.reserveamerica.com

Facilities: Water, flush toilets, coin-operated showers

Parking: At parking lot

Fee: $18; $8.65 nonrefundable reservation fee

Elevation: Near sea level

Restrictions:

  Pets—Allowed; $1 fee

  Fires—In fire rings

  Vehicles—Only 2 vehicles per site

  Other—No tent pitching in green areas; no sleeping in vehicles in parking lot

To get there: from San Francisco, drive 78 miles south on CA 1 to Santa Cruz. Then drive south on CA 1 to the San Andreas Road Exit. Drive south to Sand Dollar Drive and follow signs to the park entrance.

THE COAST

MONTANA DE ORO STATE PARK

Los Osos

After a week, smoggy Los Angeles seems full of snarling attack dogs and urbanites ready to carve your liver out over a parking space. But, drive north of Santa Barbara where the air is clear and you'll see hikers on cliffs at sunset, parents with babies in backpacks, ball-chasing lab retrievers, and unattended bicycles—especially at Montana de Oro State Park. Its azure, rocky coves feel like Greece; the sandwiched cliffs jutting out over the ocean remind you of Cornwall; and the long sand dunes resemble Provincetown on the Cape. With 7 miles of spectacular coast, this is one of California's largest state parks.

Montano de Oro was Chumash Indian territory until the Spanish Mission Period. The Chumash were missionized, then left without a way of life when the missions were secularized. Then came the Pechos, a Spanish family who dealt in cattle, and the ranching Spooners. Then Alexander Hazard planted hundreds of eucalyptus trees here in hopes of selling them to the railroad for ties. Hazard's lumber dreams hit the same rocks as those of other Southern California eucalyptus timber barons. The trees grew fast, but the tree grain spindled, making it useless—even as firewood.

Some thought the wrong variety of eucalyptus was imported from Australia, but not so. Botanists have determined that eucalyptus planted in California has no natural pests, so it grows so fast it spin-

CAMPGROUND RATINGS

Beauty:	★★★★★
Site privacy:	★★
Site spaciousness:	★★★
Quiet:	★★
Security:	★★★★★
Cleanliness/upkeep:	★★★★★

Montana De Oro State Park offers year-round camping with 7 miles of virgin California coast. You'll find good spring hiking and prime family tent camping.

dles. In Australia, insects slow trees' growth so that their trunks don't spindle.

Today, Montana de Oro State Park begins at the Morro Rock and goes south along a huge sandspit, some 85 feet high. This is a prime area for hiking, picnicking, sunbathing, and swimming. You can get lost in little, private, sandy hollows in the dunes. On one side, you can see the sea, and on the other, Morro Bay, the largest, least disturbed saltwater marsh in California. Bring a big backpack crammed with a

blanket, water, food, and sunscreen, because the sandspit is an all-day affair.

Farther south, the sandspit gives way to more dunes that fall off to cliffs, flat sheet rock, and small cove beaches below. Park on Pecho Valley Road above at turnouts and hike over the dune and down. Again, bring supplies, because once you get down there, you won't want to leave.

Finally, from Park Headquarters south is an ancient wave-cut terrace with sharp, upended cliffs of Monterey Shale that fall abruptly to the sea. Here and there, you'll spot accessible coves offering more sun-bathing and wading (at low tide only). Don't miss Corallina Cove, about a mile south of the Ranch House Visitor Center. At low tide, you can spot the plants and animals that live in the tidal pools. Obtain a free pamphlet and tidal schedule at the Visitor Center before you go.

East, off the coast, the park takes in about 8,000 acres of prime hiking, including Valencia Peak at 1,347 feet. From here, you can see the whole sweep of coast from Vandenberg Air Force Base (64 miles) in the south to Piedras Blancas (80 miles) in the north. I think Montana de Oro provides the best spring hiking in California. By summer, it is too hot.

The two-loop campground is in the canyon just behind Spooner Cove, where big sailing ships once unloaded supplies and took on hides and tallow (for candles). Here, the canyon is narrow and runs along Islay Creek, which Spooner dammed up to run a water wheel for power. All traffic goes by the neck of the canyon. It gets busy, so the best camping is in the back loop. As a trade-off, you'll have a longer walk to the beach from the back. Weekends are busy in the summer, so reserve early.

Camping in the canyon is close, but the atmosphere is friendly. The Ranger Station is right by the H.Q. and the Information Center, staffed by friendly locals. The Montana de Oro Campground makes you feel warm and safe. In the summer, count on lots of children. This means bicycles, skate boards, in-line skates, and the trill of youthful voices. Montana de Oro is a prime family tent camping vacation spot. If you can't handle that, head for the walk-in environmental campsites scattered in the park.

There is tap water. However, it is so heavily chlorinated it is useful for washing only, so bring drinking water. Also, bring one of those plastic bag showers to hang in a tree and sluice the sand and salt off. It wouldn't be a bad idea to bring a bucket to set by the tent for dipping sandy feet and a brush and dust pan to keep sand out of your tent.

To get there: from L.A., drive north on CA 101 to the outskirts of San Luis Obispo. Turn left on Los Osos Valley Road and drive west to Los Osos where the road becomes Pecho Valley Road. Continue south 5 miles to Montana de Oro State Park.

KEY INFORMATION

Montana de Oro State Park c/o San Luis Obispo Coast Area
20–A Higuera Street
San Luis Obispo, CA 93401

Operated by: California Department of Parks and Recreation

Information: (805) 528-0513; http://parks.ca.gov

Open: All year

Individual sites: 50

Each site has: Picnic table, fireplace

Registration: At Old Spooner Ranch Headquarters; reserve by phone, (800) 444-7275, or online, www.reserveamerica.com (available in summer only)

Facilities: Heavily chlorinated tap water, pit toilets

Parking: At site

Fee: $10 ($11 on weekends); $8.65 nonrefundable reservation fee

Elevation: Near sea level

Restrictions:

Pets—On leash only; not allowed on trails

Fires—In fireplaces

Vehicles—RVs up to 24 feet

MORRO BAY STATE PARK

Morro Bay

This campground is on Morro Bay, the last natural estuary in California. The bay is gorgeous. A snow white dune field on the horizon encloses the bay, and the luscious mud flats exposed by low tide are filled with feeding birds. You'll see scaups, grebes, goldeneyes, and buffleheads, as well as the more prosaic gulls and scoters—mostly in the winter months, from November to March. Bring field glasses and a bird book. On Los Osos Creek, 50 yards from the campground, a small marina rents canoes, rowboats, and the like for exploring the bay. It is safe sailing and makes a wonderful adventure for kids.

Outside the dunes, the ocean thuds against the sand like the beat of a huge heart. During the winter months, the Monterey pines and eucalyptus around the campground are alive with monarch butterflies. As a flock, the monarchs make long-distance migratory round-trips between Canada and the Sierra Madre of Central Mexico. Gliding on the wind, at altitudes of 10,000 feet, the monarchs find their way by using sun orientation—an ability used by migratory birds, whales, and salmon.

The last time I camped at Morro in January, I went looking for the monarchs in the eucalyptus around 8 or 9 A.M. At first, I didn't see them. Then, they appeared! Butterflies in clusters so thick I could barely make out the eucalyptus leaves. As the day

CAMPGROUND RATINGS

Beauty: ★★★
Site privacy: ★★
Site spaciousness: ★★★
Quiet: ★★
Security: ★★★★
Cleanliness/upkeep: ★★★★

At Morro Bay State Park, you'll find great off-season camping situated on wonderful Morro Bay. Be sure to make reservations for the summer or for holiday weekends.

warmed up, the monarchs disengaged and fluttered above me. In a short time, the sky was full of swirling butterflies. They feed off the eucalyptus bloom. Their diet is 90% water and 10% nectar. In the afternoon, as the day cooled, monarchs returned to the trees and gathered in dense clusters to stay warm during the night.

When the monarchs migrate from the cooler north and the mountains to the warm central coast, the male flies in spirals around the female of his choice and gives off an attractive scent. The female monarch may accept his overtures by following him to a protected place. There, the male struts in front of her, opening and closing his wings. If all goes well, the pair mate.

Afterward, the female looks for a milkweed plant where she will lay her eggs. The larvae eat their way out of their casings and feast on the milkweed so heartily that their weight increases 2,700 times until they metamorph into mature monarchs and fly away.

The campground is heavily used in the summer and on holidays. Fall, winter, and spring are the best times to visit (and to see the monarchs). The area is friendly and safe. By the marina, you'll find a good outdoor cafe for lunch or coffee. On the headland, visit the museum staffed by extremely helpful volunteers who are knowledgeable about the area.

The campsites feel close and safe under huge trees. A golf course runs along one side. There are flush toilets and coin-operated showers. Since Morro Bay is pretty far from any major urban center, campers have that bonhomie of folks accustomed to being on the road.

The town of Morro Bay is just around the shore with a battery of alluring fish restaurants on the waterfront. We opted for a fresh fish purchase from the fish market to be grilled on the campsite barbecue. (Wood is for sale at the camp office.) Locals tell me the cafe on the pier in Cayucas, a little town just up the coast, is a prime spot for good, fresh food.

The Morro Bay region is still in a state of grace. There are weeks of wonderful things to do. The natural scenery is as pristine as it can get, and the people who live there are friendly toward tourists. The restaurants are fun and affordable. The fishing is incredible. It's a wonderful year-round place to go.

To **get there:** from L.A., take U.S. 101 north to San Luis Obisbo (about 200 miles). Take CA 1 north 13 miles to South Bay Boulevard, then 0.7 mile to the park entrance. Or, from the town of Morro Bay, go to the south end of Main Street. Watch carefully for the entrance to the park, since it is not very well signed.

THE COAST

POINT MUGU STATE PARK

Big Sycamore Canyon, Near Oxnard

A school of dolphins pushing bait fish into the shore, working them around the rocky points—dolphin skin wet black against the blue water—that was my first impression of Point Mugu State Park's Big Sycamore Canyon Campground. The beach is gorgeous, a white sand jewel of a place to picnic, sun, and swim on an unspoiled stretch of coastline.

Later, I discovered that the Chumash Native Americans once lived in the canyon and believed that dolphins were their brothers. At one time, the Chumash lived on over-populated islands to the west. Legend has it that their mother god told them to cross over the sea to the mainland by walking on a rainbow. The caveat was that they couldn't look down. Of course, some did and fell into the sea. But, the mother god took pity on them and turned them into dolphins.

The Chumash fished from canoes 25 feet long, lashed with sinew and caulked with asphalt from seeps. They gathered clams, oysters, and abalone along the shores and made soapstone bows inlaid with mother of pearl from the shells. They hunted and gathered food in the upper reaches of the canyon and lived a life of ease, culture, and bounty. However, the Spanish put a quick end to that, and now we can camp where they lived at the mouth of the canyon, where it is cool in the summer and warm in the winter.

CAMPGROUND RATINGS

Beauty: ★★★★★
Site privacy: ★★
Site spaciousness: ★★★
Quiet: ★★★
Security: ★★★★★
Cleanliness/upkeep: ★★★★★

Big Sycamore Canyon Campground offers beautiful vistas of the sea, the sky, and the canyon. Just outside Los Angeles, Point Mugu State Park is a jewel.

Like Malibu Creek State Park, Point Magu State Park and Big Sycamore Canyon Campground are heavily used, both for overnight camping and for day use. Buses of school kids come for the morning. Mountain bikers access the fire roads up in the canyon. And many hikers come for the wildflowers. Still, the pristine beaches, rolling hills, savannah meadows, and the glorious canyon so close to the Greater Los Angeles Metropolitan Area, make Big Sycamore Canyon a must-visit campground.

Try to visit in the off-season, but watch the weather in order to schedule the best hiking days. Or, reserve ahead and hit the beach in the summer. The canyon is cool enough in summer for biking. Prime surf fishing is available off Thornhill Broome State Beach, just up the road. You can buy bait just south at Neptune's Net.

This is an excellent area for viewing monarch butterflies. They clump in the sycamore in the canyon and eat milkweed up in the meadows. Why don't sea gulls just descend on the easily spotted, brightly decorated monarchs and have a big chow-down? Because milkweed is poisonous. Rasputin used it to knock off other members of the Russian court. Milkweed is toxic enough so that when birds pick up a milkweed-eating monarch, they feel sick and learn to leave them alone. The monarch's bright colors serve to alert the birds to eat at their own risk.

In Big Sycamore Canyon, you'll find many sycamores. You'll also find coast live oak and areas of chaparral and coastal shrub. Look for blue elderberry, wild rose, California bay, purple sage, and, of course, poison oak. Make a habit of washing your hands and other exposed areas with dish detergent after a hike, and don't swim in any stream or stream-fed pond after even a gentle rain. The oil from the poison oak gets in the water and will make you very unhappy.

Like Malibu Creek State Park, there is a Ranger Headquarters at Point Magu State Park, near Big Sycamore Campground. The park feels safe, well regulated, and well patrolled, which is comforting so close to dense urban areas. If you tire of Point Mugu's small beach, remember there are miles of beaches just a short drive away. The aforementioned Neptune's Net, just south of the campground, is a good place to eat fish and chips or buy crab or lobster to grill. On some weekends, the outdoor patio restaurant can be overrun with biker gangs. Of course, upon close examination, the bikers look and act like very well-behaved middle-class Americans (and probably are!). They fit right in with the younger surfers and us middle-aged campers.

You must *plan* a visit to Point Mugu and Big Sycamore Canyon. Watch the weather and avoid the June blahs. Beware of weather predictions calling for "early-morning and late-afternoon fog along the coastline." And don't forget to make reservations. Don't expect the actual campground itself to be too scenic. Look to the sea, the sky, and the canyon for incredible vistas.

KEY INFORMATION

Big Sycamore Canyon Campground, Point Mugu State Park

Angeles District

1925 Las Virgenes Road Calabasas, CA 91302

Operated by: California Department of Parks and Recreation

Information: (818) 880-0350; http://parks.ca.gov

Open: All year

Individual sites: 54

Each site has: Picnic tables, fire grills

Registration: At entrance; reserve by phone, (800) 444-7275, or online, reserveamerica.com

Facilities: Water, flush toilets, showers

Parking: At site

Fee: $14–18; $8.65 nonrefundable reservation fee

Elevation: Sea level

Restrictions:

Pets—Allowed

Fires—Allowed (no wood gathering)

Vehicles—RVs up to 31 feet

To get there: from L.A., drive 32 miles north up CA 1 or drive 16 miles south of Oxnard.

THE COAST

VENTANA CAMPGROUND
Big Sur

Henry Miller, the famous author, washed up in beautiful Big Sur after a long life of roaming the world and was suitably impressed. He describes Big Sur's majesty as "almost painful to behold. That prehistoric look. The look of always. Nature smiling at herself in the mirror of eternity." The Spanish named the country *el país grande del sur* or big country to the south—*Big Sur.*

Big Sur is about 80 miles of rugged Santa Lucia Mountains slashed by canyons and gorges that fall hundreds of feet into a wild emerald sea full of otters, sea lions, and whales. There are beach cliffs of jade, streams clear as glass, and the world's largest trees, the coastal redwoods. In winter it rains, and in summer morning fogs burn off by noon and highs average 70°F.

The first white settler in Big Sur was George Davis (1853). He had a spat with his wife in Monterey and moved down on the Big Sur River, which runs though Pfeiffer Big Sur State Park and Andrew Molera State Park. After eight years, he cooled off and moved home. Then came a trickle of others—Michael and Barbara Pfeiffer on the side-wheeler *Nevada* and William and Anselma Post who packed in their stoves and beds on mule-driven wagons.

Most of this incredible stretch of CA 1 was built by convicts from San Quentin and Folsom, who lived in work camps at Little Sur River, Anderson Creek, and

CAMPGROUND RATINGS

Beauty:	★★★★★
Site privacy:	★★★★★
Site spaciousness:	★★★★★
Quiet:	★★★★★
Security:	★★★★★
Cleanliness/upkeep:	★★★★★

At Ventana Campground you'll find luxury tent camping nestled in the towering trees on Big Sur.

Salem Creek. They picked up a princely $2.50 per day for pick and shovel labor. Though the work was grueling, the men loved the chance to be outside. And the Department of Corrections claimed that it prepared the men "for return to free society—both physically and psychologically." It took nine years for the convicts and underpaid Chinese laborers to finish the Carmel–San Simeon Highway.

The tourist business started in about 1902 when Florence Pfeiffer grew plenty tired of the stream of guests lounging around Pfeiffer Ranch with her husband, John. She finally cracked when one guest hit a mule with a stick. From then on, her husband's friends were required to pay $3 per day for room and board, or they would be asked to leave. Now, the tourist business is booming. The traffic on CA 1 is often constant, and the campgrounds are jammed, especially in the summer.

Only lovely Ventana Campground seems to have any available sites. Ventana is located in the redwoods below Ventana Inn on a 40-acre piece of land once owned by the Posts. The campground is now owned by the Inn. All the sites are situated on the mountainside, so as to give each site maximum privacy, view, and space. The forest floor is clean and soft—great for tent camping. And indeed, Ventana caters to tent campers. It is clean and well regulated—a perfect place to enjoy Big Sur.

You can hike behind the Ventana Inn on fire roads, but the best hiking is down in Pfeiffer Big Sur State Park near Ventana Campground. The State Park has 821 acres and 6 hiking trails ranging from a 20-minute stroll to a 4-mile, 2-

hour hike. The stream that runs through the park, Big Sur River, is perfect for wading during most times of year.

While hiking, keep an eye out for wild pigs. Apparently, hunters introduced the wild boar back at the turn of the century for sport. The boars weigh about 300 pounds and sport some nasty tusks. They are nocturnal and feed at twilight on bulbs and roots. One hungry sow can rip up a hundred square yards of meadow in one night. They have piglets in the spring, and that's when their disposition turns especially ugly. It's best to steer clear of them.

Just north of the Ventana Campground turnoff is Sycamore Canyon Road, which leads to Pfeiffer Beach. This beach is usually not signed—the locals have a time-honored tradition of chainsawing off the signpost leading to their local beach. However, the natives are not churlish about sharing the sand and incredible view.

In fact, I found the natives to be surprisingly good-natured and friendly. There was a big movement to close CA 1 off to tourists at one time. Then, nature did it for them in 1983 with a huge mudslide between Julia Pfeiffer Burns State Park and Partington Ridge. It closed the road for more than a year and took 150 men and women working 7 days a week with 30 bulldozers and 7,700 pounds of explosives to clear the road. The closure hit the area hard causing layoffs and cutbacks, and most locals realized that no matter how beautiful Big Sur is, it's the tourists who put hay in the barn.

To get there: from Carmel, drive 30 miles south on CA 1. Ventana Campground is on the left just past Pfeiffer Big Sur State Park.

KEY INFORMATION

Ventana Campground
P.O. Box 206
Big Sur, CA 93920
Operated by: Ventana in Big Sur

Information: (831) 667-2688; www.ventanabigsur.com

Open: All year

Individual sites: 75

Each site has: Picnic table, fire ring

Registration: At entrance; for reservations, call or send $25 to the above address, two weeks in advance, with a letter noting site number desired and dates of stay and a stamped, self-addressed envelope for a return confirmation letter

Facilities: Water, hot coin-operated showers

Parking: At site

Fee: $25 (1 vehicle, 2 people); $5 per extra person; $5 per extra vehicle

Elevation: 400 feet

Restrictions:

Pets—On leash only; $5 fee for dogs

Fires—In fire rings (firewood available)

Vehicles—No RVs over 22 feet

Other—Personal checks not accepted

SOUTHERN CALIFORNIA

THE DESERT

THE DESERT

ARROYO SALADO PRIMITIVE CAMPGROUND

Anza-Borrego Desert State Park

A rroyo Salado is badlands camping. It is in malpais (bad country) in the huge Anza-Borrego Desert State Park (ABDSP), which has everything—palm-studded canyons, cactus gardens, mountain pinyon forests, hot springs, waterfalls, bighorn sheep, Native American pictographs and petroglyphs, historic emigrant trails, stage stops, and ghost towns. A good way to come into Arroyo Salado is on CA 86, off I-10, via Indio and Coachella through the date palm orchards. Stop and have a date shake at one of the stands. Then, carry on along the shore past Salton City Beach and turn east on S-22. Notice Travertine Point on the right and the wave terraces cut into the mountainsides—in recent geological times, the Salton basin was a huge lake. Near the wave terraces are traces of the Native Americans who lived by the lake.

Now, you're in the malpais. This area is characterized by abrupt gullies with banks of sun-hardened clay, gravel-strewn sand, and strange shapes of clay. Red and yellow are the prevailing colors, with mud-hued grays and drabs for a background. After the winter rains, all the flowers bloom—flame-tipped ocotillo, verbena, desert sunflower, lavender, brittlebush, creosote bush, primrose, teddy bear cholla, and beavertail cactus. The entrance to the Arroyo Salado primitive camping area is 11.8 miles on the left (or, from the opposite

CAMPGROUND RATINGS

Beauty: ★★★★★
Site privacy: ★★★★★
Site spaciousness: ★★★★★
Quiet: ★★★★★
Security: ★
Cleanliness/upkeep: ★★★★

Arroyo Salado Primitive Campground is situated in malpais, with lizards, flowers, and the rainbow colors of the dunes. It's for the hardcore tent camper seeking a unique experience; not for young children.

direction, 19 miles from the Park H.Q. in Borrego Springs). The campground is marked by a metal sign reading "Arroyo Salado." As with all the signs in ABDSP, it is small and unannounced, so you have to be on your toes to see it. Often, there is a turnaround past the entrance to make reapproaching a little easier.

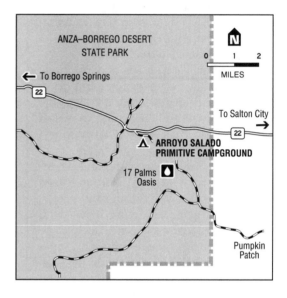

An often sandy road goes down the wash with various turnoffs where you can park your car and camp. Carry your tent up over the hummocks, and, suddenly, you'll be alone in untracked malpais. Everywhere is a good place to pitch a tent. The desert floor is clean and sandy. Sit down and listen to the wind and look for lizards flitting over the rocks and dunes. Wait, and the desert comes to you.

The road continues down to 17 Palms Oasis, Una Palma, and Five Palms. None of these places has the number of palms their names advertise, but there is a spring at 17 Palms, as well as a visitor's register consisting of a wooden keg full of notes lodged in the palm fronds of two adjoining palm trees. This desert post office was begun by early-day travelers and prospectors. These considerate travelers also left a fresh water supply for those who followed. The saline water here is drinkable, although highly laxative. In the early 1900s, the famous British traveler J. Smeaton Chase came this way and noted that "rice boiled in it was thoroughly disgusting in color and taste; no amount of sugar could render it more than just bearable. The tea had a dirty gray curdle and a flavor like bilge, and when I tried cocoa as an alternative the mixture promptly went black."

Past 17 Palms, the road continues south and connects with a network of roads in the Borrego Badlands. Don't go any farther unless you have a four-wheel-drive vehicle in good shape and lots of water. You can camp anywhere you want in ABDSP as long as you don't park more than ten feet off established dirt roads. Of course, you must carry out your garbage. However, the recent, welcome addition of a vault toilet spares campers the task of burying waste. No fires are allowed, unless you bring in wood and burn it in a metal container—a portable barbecue would be fine.

Remember, carry a lot of water; one gallon per day per person should do it. It's not a bad idea to carry a collapsible shovel or sawed-off gardening shovel. If you get stuck in sand, it will be your best friend. Bring some old sheets and light rope. You can sit on one sheet and rig another for shade using the rope. Sleep under a sheet early in the night and get in your sleeping bag later when it gets cold.

To resupply or escape the heat, go to Borrego Springs, where they sell grapefruit and oranges under shade trees on the traffic circle. Just up Palm Canyon Drive is the Visitor Center where you can buy maps and books and see exhibits. There is an easy 3-mile round-trip nature trail up Borrego Palm Canyon leaving from the Palm Canyon Campground one mile from the Visitor Center. Enjoy the parks more than 400,000 dessert acres.

> **To get there:** from L.A., take I-10 east to CA 86. Head south to the junction with S-22 near Salton City. Turn right and travel 11.8 miles to the entrance on the left.
>
> Or, take I-10 east to I-15 south to Temecula. Take CA 79 to the junction with S-2 past Warner Springs. Take S-2 to S-22 to Borrego Springs and the ABDSP Visitor Center. Drive 19 miles east of the Visitor Center on S-22 to the campground.

KEY INFORMATION

Arroyo Salado Primitive Campground
Anza-Borrego Desert State Park
200 Palm Canyon Drive
Borrego Springs, CA 92004

Operated by: California Department of Parks and Recreation

Information: (760) 767-5311; http://parks.ca.gov

Open: All year (avoid summer)

Individual sites: Open area

Each site has: No facilities

Registration: Not required

Facilities: Vault toilet; bring plenty of water

Parking: Some pullouts; otherwise, less than 10 feet off established dirt roads.

Fee: None

Elevation: 880 feet

Restrictions:

Pets—On six-foot or shorter leash only; must stay in tent or vehicle overnight; not allowed on trails or in wilderness

Fires—In portable barbecues only

Vehicles—Suited for pickup-campers

Other—Don't camp near water holes, since wildlife depend on them for water; all vegetation (even dead wood) is protected

THE DESERT

CULP VALLEY PRIMITIVE CAMPGROUND

Anza-Borrego Desert State Park

Culp Valley Primitive Campground is perched high in the San Ysidro Mountains overlooking the Borrego Valley. It's a good choice for late spring when it is too hot in the valley below and the wildflowers are still in bloom higher up. In winter or early spring, Culp Valley may be too cold and windy for comfortable camping.

The mountains of Culp Valley are composed of old granite, and the exposed peaks and hills have eroded into huge piles of granite boulders scattered around the meadows. The trees found in this area are California juniper, sumac, scrub oak, mountain mahogany, and silk-tassel bush. The meadows were covered with tiny flowers when I was there in March. Spring was happening slower in the mountains at 3,400 feet than it was down in the Borrego Valley, where the flowers were in full bloom.

As you pull into the campground, there is a dirt road to the left—the California Riding and Hiking Trail. You'll find good pullout spots a few hundred yards up the trail with places to pitch a tent that have full views of the Borrego Valley below. More places to camp are in the regular campground ahead. You'll have no problem parking, but the challenge is finding a flat area to pitch a tent. I parked, carried my tent about 50 yards up into the meadow, and pitched it on a nice grassy area filled with wildflowers. It wasn't quite flat,

CAMPGROUND RATINGS

Beauty:	★★★★★
Site privacy:	★★★★★
Site spaciousness:	★★★★★
Quiet:	★★★★★
Security:	★
Cleanliness/upkeep:	★★★★

Culp Valley Primitive Campground provides cool camping when ABDSP heats up. Good for birding and great hiking through bighorn sheep country. With no facilities, Culp Valley is for the hardcore tent camper who doesn't mind carrying gear away from the car. Not recommended for children

but as long as my head was up and my feet down, I had no problem sleeping. Watch for gopher holes and ant hills as well.

Pena Spring is 0.75 mile west of the campground. Follow the west fork of the Culp Valley Campground access road 0.3 mile to the parking area. Then, walk down the old road until it dead-ends. A few yards to the west is the spring. Bring binoculars, as Pena Spring is a great birding spot, especially when water is hard to find, and the birds must travel to Pena Spring to get it.

From the campground, a 0.6-mile trail leads to an overlook of the Borrego Valley. I walked up at dusk and caught the whole floor below me, as well as the blue of the Salton Sea on the horizon. In Old Pegleg Smith's days, there was no Salton Sea—just the floor of an ancient sea and a few salt companies that worked the dry alkali basin. Land speculators had dreamed of irrigating the Imperial Valley south of the Salton Sea and starting a land rush. In 1901, their dreams came true. Sluice gates opened on the Colorado River and diverted water through canals and ditches into the valley. It was a modern engineering miracle.

Then, in 1905, the Colorado River broke through the main canal and ran wild, inundating towns, smashing bridges, and flowing into the Salton Basin. Thousands of Native American and Mexican laborers fought the flood, and the Southern Pacific Railroad drove freight trains filled with rock into the breach. Finally, the Colorado River subsided, leaving a permanent saline lake, the Salton Sea, one of our nation's first environmental disasters.

Another good hike is down the California Hiking and Riding Trail about 8 miles into the valley below. I thought I saw a bighorn sheep about halfway down, but, by the time I got out my binoculars, it was gone. The trail dead-ends at the Park Visitor Center.

I desperately wanted a close-up view of a bighorn. I once read an account by a hiker in which he described the bighorns' eyes. "Their eyes are a clear, golden amber with a long oval, velvety black pupil." Keen sighted, the bighorn can pick out the stealthy movements of a mountain lion from miles away. They can bound and run like the wind. Their specially adapted hooves have bottoms that cling to smooth surfaces and edges that cut into snow or ice and gain a purchase on the smallest projections of the rocks. The bighorn is truly a remarkable animal.

Three-quarters of a mile down the road from the Culp Valley Campground is the Culp Valley Road (dirt) on the right, which leads to the Culp Valley Picnic Area. Follow the dirt road about 0.5 mile west, then make a left turn through big boulders to the picnic area. This is a really nice spot, and I've rarely met anyone else there. I understand the picnic area is built on the old homesite of an early cattle rancher.

To get there: from L.A., take I-10 east to I-15. Go south to Temecula. Take CA 79 east to the junction with S-2 just past Warner Springs. Turn left on S-2. Go left again on S-22. The Culp Valley Salado Primitive Campground is on the left, 9.3 miles from your CA 79 turnoff.

KEY INFORMATION

Culp Valley Primitive Campground, Anza-Borrego Desert State Park
200 Palm Canyon Drive
Borrego Springs, CA 92004

Operated by: California Department of Parks and Recreation

Information: (760) 767-5311; http://parks.ca.gov

Open: All year (avoid summer heat)

Individual sites: Open area

Each site has: No facilities

Registration: Not required

Facilities: Vault toilet; bring plenty of water

Parking: Some pullouts; otherwise, don't park more than 10 feet off established dirt roads.

Fee: none

Elevation: 3,400 feet

Restrictions:

Pets—On 6-foot leash or shorter only; must stay in tent or vehicle overnight; not allowed on trails or in wilderness

Fires—In portable barbecues only

Vehicles—Suited for pickup campers

Other—Don't camp near water holes, since wildlife depend on them for water; all vegetation (even dead wood) is protected

THE DESERT

LITTLE BLAIR VALLEY PRIMITIVE CAMPGROUND

Anza-Borrego Desert State Park

In the middle of March, I camped in Little Blair Valley on the edge of a tremendous meadow. The moon was so full that the tiny flowers sparkled from between the startlingly green grass. What a night!

I was alone until morning when a couple drove by in a rental car. They were lost and looking for the Native American pictographs. We consulted his map, then they were off in a cloud of dust. The rest of the morning it was just me, watching the sun move across the valley and rocks .

The S-2 turnoff to Little Blair Valley is 4 miles south of Scissors Crossing, about 31 miles from ABDSP H.Q. in Borrego Springs. On the left, you'll see the tiny stake sign embossed with "Little Blair." The road, usually passable by all passenger cars, goes a mile or so over a ridge into the valley. Here, you'll encounter another stake sign indicating the S-2 highway from which you just came. To the left is a wonderful area for camping in the soft meadow grass.

The road to the right of the S-2 marker curls around the edge of the valley passing several turnouts with many promising spots for parking and camping. Before you pick one, think about how the sun will travel and when you want to be in the shade or sun.

From here, three short, good hikes are within easy range. Drive up to the head of Little Blair Valley and you'll see another

CAMPGROUND RATINGS

Beauty: ★★★★★
Site privacy: ★★★★★
Site spaciousness: ★★★★★
Quiet: ★★★★★
Security: ★★
Cleanliness/upkeep: ★★★★★

Little Blair Valley is primitive tent camping in a valley full of wildflowers and Native American pictographs and mortreros. Plan a trip in the spring and bring water.

stake signing the Morteros. There is a parking area and a short 0.75-mile trail leading to large rocks filled with Native American grinding holes. With these morteros, women pulverized coarse seeds and pods, such as mesquite beans, and made a pulp to be dried in the sun and used later for bread. Also, fine seeds and delicate plant parts were rubbed or lightly ground on smooth, polished patches of rock, known as slicks. The trail continues another mile or so east through a ruggedly beautiful canyon.

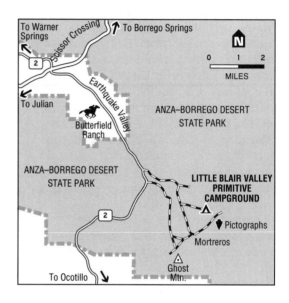

From the Morteros parking lot, you can also follow a sign 0.1 mile to the Pictograph Trail. Usually passable, the 1.5-mile dirt road leads to the Pictograph parking lot. From there, climb a ridge and go down the other side to a huge boulder painted in geometric red and yellow designs. Notice the different vegetation—juniper, white sage, and pinyon pine.

Go past the pictographs and see more Native American morteros at the base of the ridge to the right. Continue down the wash and into Smuggler Canyon. When the canyon makes a sharp turn to the right, you'll see the Vallecito Valley and the Vallecito Stage Station from the edge of a steep drop.

Smuggler Canyon got its name from the Chinese laborers who came by boat from China, via the Sea of Cortez, to Mexicali. They were then smuggled up to the canyon to avoid law enforcement and angry locals. Once past the frontier, they worked in mines and on farms and railroads. A strenuous hike down Smuggler Canyon will lead you to S-2, a few hundred yards east of Vallecito Stage Station. Arrange a pickup there, since the return is heavy going.

Drive 2 miles past the Morteros pull-out into the Blair Valley (not Little Blair Valley), and you'll see a signed turn to the left going to the Marshall South Home on Ghost Mountain. Park in the lot just down the road and hike 1 mile straight up the mountain to see the ruins of the house.

In 1932, Marshall South and his wife, Tanya, built a house on top of the beautiful Ghost Mountain, which they called "Yaquitepec." They saved rain-water in cisterns and ate yucca and agave like the local Native Americans. Supplies were brought in by Model-T from the town of Julian and carried up the mountain by mule or man. Marshall and Tanya raised three children and supported themselves by writing for *Desert Magazine*. Finally, in a phrase that sends a chill down the spine of every married man, Tanya "tired of the eccentricities of her husband" and moved to San Diego, where she remarried.

From the parking lot, you can drive back to S-2 through Blair Valley, passing several pullouts and some good camping sites. Blair Valley is regularly trafficked by RVers and tent campers. However, it is a good idea to check with the ABDSP H.Q. on the condition of the roads, especially after a rain.

There is a good restaurant up the road at Butterfield Ranch, where I had an excellent enchilada. There is a convenience store nearby as well.

To get there: from L.A., take I-10 east to I-15. Go south to Temecula. Take CA 79 east past Warner Springs to Julian. From Julian on CA 79 drive 12 miles east to S-2. Go right 4 miles on S-2 and find the stake marker "Little Blair" on the left. Follow the dirt road about a mile to Little Blair Valley.

MESQUITE SPRINGS CAMPGROUND

Death Valley National Park

On your way to Mesquite Springs, stop at the legendary Mad Greek's Restaurant in Baker for the lunch of your life. The souvlaki is unforgettable. However, if you can't bear Greek, there is a park with shaded picnic tables in town. Remember, your last chance to fuel up is 51 miles from the campground in Furnace Creek.

Despite its morbid name, Death Valley is a pretty lively place. For thousands of years Native Americans lived on the shores of successive lakes that filled the basin. When the last lake dried up, the nomadic Shoshone camped in the valley near the springs in the winter and in the mountains in the heat of the summer. For the last thousand years, they lived on the ample game, mesquite beans, and pinyon nuts.

It took an overly eager forty-niner to dub the bountiful valley "Death Valley." He was one of a group of impatient argonauts who ignored their experienced wagon master and took a Native American trail in hopes of shaving miles off the trip. The group wound up bogged down in the sand around Furnace Creek. When rescued, the forty-niner theatrically exclaimed, "Goodbye, Death Valley," as he turned his back on his own folly.

Seeing Death Valley for the first time is like seeing the earth without clothes. Immense land forms, volcanic craters, and rainbowed landscapes of salt flats and snow-capped mountains cover the area.

CAMPGROUND RATINGS

Beauty: ★★★★★
Site privacy: ★
Site spaciousness: ★★★★
Quiet: ★★★★
Security: ★★★★★
Cleanliness/upkeep: ★★★★★

This campground in Death Valley National Park is one of the few not overrun by large snowbird RVs in the winter. Don't come here in the summer—Death Valley is one of the hottest places on earth.

There are original water springs, Ice Age fish, ghost towns, lost mines, plants found nowhere else in the world, and even a Spanish-Moorish castle, Scotty's Castle, built in the middle of nowhere.

Below Scotty's Castle lies the Mesquite Springs Campground, set in the Grapevine Canyon wash. It has spring water spigots, flush toilets, and well-maintained tent/RV sites with fireplaces and tables. You'll find soft, sandy spots to pitch your tent and a beautiful view of the entire valley with snow-covered Telescope Peak rising 11,000 feet in the south.

Far enough from Stovepipe Wells and the golf course at Furnace Creek, Mesquite Springs Campground is not heavily camped except during Easter holiday. Still, it's not a bad idea to phone the Ranger Station near the campground at (760) 786-2331 to check on availability. It's a hefty drive back to Furnace Creek and the Texas Spring campground, which is your alternative. Remember too, that the only supplies in Death Valley are sold in Furnace Creek and Stovepipe Wells.

A visit to Scotty's Castle is a half-day affair. After the guided tour, the bookstore, and a stroll around the grounds, find the tree-shaded picnic tables for lunch. Nearby is Ubehebe Crater and Little Hebe, which constitute another half-day excursion.

In Death Valley, distance shrinks. The locals think nothing of driving 60 miles for a cup of coffee. In that spirit, the ghost town of Rhyolite and Beatty with its gambling casinos (64 miles away) are just around the corner, as are the mining towns of Tonopah and Goldfield.

Hiking around Mesquite Springs Campground is fun. Because of the terrain, it's almost impossible to get lost. Still, always take a lot of water with you, even if you are just going out for a stroll. The last time we camped there it was a full moon, and we could see the entire valley far below us gleaming in the light. From the trees near the spring, an owl swooped down and rose again with a little creature in its claws. What a magical night!

This is a good campground for children. The campground roads are easily navigable and safe, so bring their bicycles. There is swimming at Stovepipe Wells and Furnace Creek. (Remember, Death Valley is long-haul driving country.) The fee is a nominal $2 per person. The water in the pool at Furnace Creek is as pure as can be. It's new water being generated inside an extinct volcano about 10 miles away.

KEY INFORMATION

Mesquite Spring Campground Death Valley National Park P.O. Box 579 Death Valley, CA 92328

Operated by: National Park Service

Information: (760) 786-2331; www.nps.gov/deva

Open: All year

Individual sites: 30

Each site has: Picnic tables, fireplaces

Registration: At entrance

Facilities: Water, flush toilets, sanitary disposal station

Parking: At individual sites

Fee: $10

Elevation: 1,800 feet

Restrictions:

Pets—On leash only

Fires—In fireplaces

Vehicles—RVs or trailers

To get there: from L.A., drive 65 miles east on I-10 to I-15. Go north 135 miles to Baker. From Baker, drive 86 miles north on CA 127 through Shoshone to Death Valley Junction. From there drive 29 miles on CA 190 to Furnace Creek. Head north 51 miles to Mesquite Springs Campground on the left just before the Ranger Station.

MID HILLS CAMPGROUND
Mojave National Preserve

The East Mojave isn't half as wild and woolly today as it was in 1826 when Jedediah Smith came through with a pack of angry Mojave Native Americans on his trail. Ambushed crossing the Colorado River, Smith lost half his trading party to Mojave war clubs before he forted up in a thicket of cottonwoods. With only five Kentucky rifles, Smith and his mountain men discouraged the Mojaves enough with pinpoint rifle fire to escape and run for their lives across the East Mojave Desert.

It was August 18 and hotter than Hades. Tormented by thirst, the men "found some relief from chewing slips of the Cabbage Pear" (Smith's diary). Men dropped from exhaustion and could not go on until water could be found and brought back to them. "It seemed a more fitting abode for fiends than any living thing that belongs to our world" (James Ohio Pattie). Traveling by night, the men spent the days by springs that Smith vaguely remembered from his trip the year before. They followed the Old Mojave Trail—a trading route used by the Mojave for hundreds of years—and passed near present-day Mid Hills Campground on their terrified flight across the desert wastes toward the Cajon Pass.

Nowadays, Mid Hills Campground is about the most pleasant place to spend some time in these parts. Set in rolling

CAMPGROUND RATINGS

Beauty:	★★★
Site privacy:	★★★★★
Site spaciousness:	★★★★
Quiet:	★★★★★
Security:	★★
Cleanliness/upkeep:	★★★

Come to Mid Hills Campground for the spring bloom. The back roads are good for mountain biking. This untracked area is spectacular!

country among juniper and pinyon pine, Mid Hills is high enough to get snow, sometimes in May. I liked site #14 for its views of the mountains through the trees and the many places to pitch a tent. Also enticing are the sites situated on the edge of a drop, with a view of the vast Cima Dome and the Kelso Dunes to the south.

Between the Providence and New York mountains, Mid Hills is the trailhead for the 8-mile hike to Hole-in-the-Wall Campground. Start at Mid Hills for a mostly downhill trek and arrange a return ride. A mile or so into the hike, there is a small cold-water seep coming from beneath a dead juniper. I can imagine Jedediah Smith and his boys lying around there in the blazing sun waiting for the Mojave to beset them.

The trail features incredible views, and the land changes quickly from the pine-juniper forest to desert—with bright, delicate desert flowers for a short while in springtime. At the end of the hike, coming up a blind canyon, there are rings set in the rock that help get you over the steep sections of the hike.

Hole-in-the-Wall Campground is the only organized alternative to Mid Hills. When both campgrounds are full, campers may tent in "previously disturbed areas." This option gives you a couple thousand beautiful campsites from which to choose. In fact, just around the corner from Hole-in-the-Wall Campground, you'll find a whole series of turnoffs on the incredibly scenic Wild Horse Canyon Road. Be sure to drive it—you'll see cholla and wildflowers growing on volcanic slopes and rocky mesa, sage, and the pinyon-juniper woodland of Mid Hills Campground.

When visiting the Mojave National Preserve, water is your paramount concern. Count on at least a gallon per person, per day. Phone the park before you leave to see which campground has water. When we visited, Hole-in-the-Wall had water, but Mid Hills didn't.

Gasoline is also scarce. Fill up when you can. It is illegal to burn anything you find in the preserve—even dead wood—so bring your own wood or charcoal. Wind is another consideration. Mid Hills is protected by trees and hills, but Hole-in-the-Wall is out in the open. Bring ear plugs if you can't sleep through the noise of a tent flapping in the breeze

Between the Mitchell Caverns (tours available weekdays at 1:30 P.M., weekends at 10 A.M. and 3 P.M.), Kelso Dunes, Cinder Cones National Natural Landmark, Cima Dome, Fort Piute, Whiskey Pete's casino, hotel, restaurant, and truck stop just across the border in Nevada, and the Mad Greek's Restaurant in Baker, you could easily spend a week around the Mojave National Preserve.

On the way to the Mojave National Preserve, stop at the California Welcome Center off I-15 (4 miles south of Barstow; (760) 253-4813) for maps, guidebooks, and information. Spring is the season to visit Mojave National Preserve. Not only are the riots of flowers in bloom, but also the desert is scoured clean by winter, leaving a crust over the sand to keep the dust down.

KEY INFORMATION

Mid Hills Campground
c/o Mojave Desert Information Center
Mojave National Preserve
P.O. Box 241
Baker, CA 92309

Operated by: National Park Service

Information: (760) 733-4040 or (760) 253-4813; www.nps.gov/moja

Open: All year (forget summer)

Individual sites: 26

Each site has: Fire rings, picnic tables

Registration: At entrance

Facilities: Pit toilets, trash cans, water (usually)

Parking: At site

Fee: $12

Elevation: 5,600 feet

Restrictions:

Pets—On leash only

Fires—In fire rings

Vehicles—2 per site (the unpaved road to the campground is unsuitable for RVs)

Other—Bring firewood/charcoal

To get there: from L.A., take I-10 east to I-15 north to I-40. Go east on I-40 near Essex, then take the Essex Road exit and drive 10 miles north to Black Canyon Road. Then drive 9 miles north following the signs to the campground.

SADDLEBACK BUTTE STATE PARK

Lancaster

Saddleback Butte State Park is little known, well run, and very convenient to the Los Angeles area. It lies just over the hill on the Antelope Freeway, an oasis in the creeping suburbia of Antelope Valley. I like the park because of its proximity to Los Angeles. It's perfect for a quick desert camping hit if you don't have time to drive to Joshua Tree National Park or Anza-Borrego Desert State Park.

The San Gabriel Mountains to the south block out the L.A. smog. You'll see wildflowers among the park's many Joshua trees from February through May. In fact, the park was once called Joshua Tree State Park, but everyone confused it with Joshua Tree National Park, so they renamed it after Saddleback Butte, a mountain a few hundred yards to the east of the campground.

Look for horned larks and alligator lizards, as well as the golden eagle, desert tortoise, and the usual compendium of desert creatures. Examine the Joshua tree, which John C. Fremont dubbed the "most repulsive tree in the vegetable kingdom" in 1844. Later, J. Smeaton Chase likened the poor tree to "a misshapen pirate with belt, boots, hands, and teeth stuck full of daggers..." Lighten up a bit, dudes. I think the *Yucca brevifolia*, as the Joshua tree is known botanically, is as beautiful as it can be and as strong as it has to be to survive in a harsh environment.

CAMPGROUND RATINGS

Beauty: ★★★
Site privacy: ★★★
Site spaciousness: ★★★
Quiet: ★★
Security: ★★★★★
Cleanliness/upkeep: ★★★★

Saddleback Butte State Park is good for a quick desert-camping hit. See the desert flowers and the museum. It's a fine first desert trip for children from Los Angeles.

DESERT

The Joshua tree is a natural supermarket. Woodrats gnaw off the lower leaves to make nests. Weevils lay eggs in the tree's terminal bud, which causes the multiple branching effect. Yucca moths are the plants' sole pollinator, and in turn, lay their eggs in the flower. Butcher birds (the loggerhead shrike) hang their prey out to dry on the sharp leaves, and woodpeckers dig holes in the limbs looking for insects. In the past, Native Americans ate the flowers, raw or roasted, and then ate the seed pods. They made sandals and carrying nets from the fiber in the leaves, and the roots were used to make dyes and medicines. In all, the Joshua tree is a useful plant. It's most beautiful in spring covered and surrounded by flowers or in winter, when the sunlight hits its tufted branches covered with snow.

The area around Saddleback Butte State Park was once antelope country. Imagine the Piute Native Americans on top of the 3,600-foot butte scouting for herds of pronghorn antelope on the distant horizon. Then came the iron horse, the railroad, in the 1870s. Not only were there hordes of trigger-happy sportsmen on the train blazing away at anything that moved, but also the pronghorn antelope had their own fatal flaw. For some reason, they couldn't cross railroad tracks. Something in the pronghorn make-up wouldn't let them. So, unable to follow their normal grazing patterns, many starved to death.

The pronghorn are among the fastest animals in the world. Three feet high at the shoulder, the pronghorn can run 65 miles per hour in short bursts and 35 miles per hour for 4 miles. There are a few left in sagebrush country on the

Modoc Plateau, but it's an uphill fight. Nobody wants a pet pronghorn antelope who can jump an eight-foot storm fence and eat the ornamentals surrounding the condo swimming pool.

The trail up Saddleback Butte starts in the campground and moves due east up an easy grade, passing through creosote and Joshua trees. It winds around the alluvial fan and climbs up the saddle-shaped hunk of granite. From the top, you can see the other buttes in the area. All of them, including Saddleback Butte, are the tops of granite mountains silted up by the alluvial plain, which is Antelope Valley. To the north is Edwards Air Force Base, and farther west are Lancaster and the Antelope Valley California Poppy Reserve, where poppies blanket entire hillsides in brilliant orange. This area is worth a visit. Remember to phone ahead at (805) 724-1180 to find out when the poppies are in bloom. From the Antelope Valley Freeway in Lancaster, take the Avenue I exit and drive 15 miles west to the reserve.

The Antelope Valley Indian Museum is also worth a stop. It is a folk museum of various Native American tribes and houses a unique southwestern collection. It is open weekends from 11 A.M. to 4 P.M., mid-September to mid-June. To get to the museum, take 170th Street 3 miles south from the Park to Avenue M. Go west for 1 mile to the museum sign. You won't regret it.

Saddleback Butte State Park is first come, first served; however, the park is only really busy one or two weekends during peak flower time in the spring. Don't camp here in the summer. October and November are pleasant times to visit. Check the weather report and wind conditions before you leave; it can really blow here. In anticipation, there are windscreens by every campsite.

KEY INFORMATION

Saddleback Butte State Park
17102 East Avenue J East
Lancaster, CA 93535

Operated by: California Department of Parks and Recreation

Information: (661) 942-0662; http://parks.ca.gov

Open: All year

Individual sites: 50; 1 reserved for groups

Each site has: Barbeque grill, picnic table, shade screens, fire rings

Registration: By entrance; reserve by phone, (800) 444-7275, or online, www.reserveamerica.com

Facilities: Water, flush toilets, dump station

Parking: At site

Fee: $8, $6 (age 62 and older); $8.65 nonrefundable reservation fee

Elevation: 2,700 feet

Restrictions:

Pets—On leash only; in campground only

Fires—In stove or fire ring

Vehicles—RVs and trailers up to 30 feet

To get there: from L.A., drive north on I-5 to I-14 north to Lancaster. Turn east on Avenue J (County Highway N5) and drive 17 miles to the park entrance.

THE DESERT

VALLECITO REGIONAL PARK

Near Anza-Borrego Desert State Park

Native Americans lived on the site of Vallecito Regional Park for thousands of years. Then came the Spanish conquistadors, Kit Carson and General Kearny, the forty-niners and the Conestoga wagons, and then, the stagecoaches. Vallecito oasis is on the main southern route westward from St. Louis, which goes through Texas to avoid mountains and bad weather. The last water is near Yuma on the Colorado River, and then there's nothing but a hundred miles of trackless, dry wasteland.

One anonymous forty-niner quoted on a park billboard describes Vallecito this way: "Imagine the weary traveler, ragged and dirty, surrounded by barren, burning sands, with no green thing upon which to rest his eye. See him toiling to ascend the sandy rise. He reaches the top and in the distance he sees the green countenance of Vallecito. Gratitude to God fills his heart when he reaches the spot where he can lie down in green pastures and refresh himself."

After ripping through the desert in an air-conditioned car, you won't get quite the same sensation, but Vallecito is truly a magical spot. Surrounded by mountains of heat-blasted rock, Vallecito is soft, green, and filled with wildlife. Behind the campground is a privately owned preserve, a mesquite forest alive with bees and birds.

The campground is simple. Under the trees, near the restored stage station and

CAMPGROUND RATINGS

Beauty: ★★★
Site privacy: ★★
Site spaciousness: ★★★
Quiet: ★★★
Security: ★★★★★
Cleanliness/upkeep: ★★★★★

Vallecito Regional Park is good for children, winter camping, and Old West lore.

cemetery on the only high ground, sit the 21 tent-only spots—well away from the RV and trailer area. The rest rooms are simple and clean. The ranger is on top of everything. This is a beautiful, well-run camp! It is a perfect place to come with children for a first-time camping trip or to frame nights spent camping in Anza-Borrego Desert State Park primitive campsites.

There is a playground for little ones. You can spot Rabbits hopping through the campground, as well as road runners, lizards, and quail. Bring binoculars and a bird book, as well as charcoal and grillables. If you forget, you can buy supplies at the two stores nearby—Butterfield Ranch and Agua Caliente. Both places also have swimming pools available for a small fee.

The reconstructed stage station is fascinating and full of history involving hauntings, lost gold, and murder. One man rode his white horse into the station one night and shot his brother dead at the bar. Another story tells of a young woman who came off the stagecoach and expired in the station. An elaborate wedding dress was found in her baggage. She was buried in it, and sometimes her apparition is seen wafting through the rooms of the stage station at dusk. Some days, hundreds of Conestoga wagons camped around the station, as the oxen and emigrants gathered strength for the final push over the mountains.

The stagecoaches ran 24 hours a day. At night a man on horseback rode ahead carrying a lantern to light the way. A six-horse team pulled the stage. There were quick stops to change horses and only one meal per day for the passengers. The 2,800-mile trip from St. Louis to San Francisco took 24 days. Imagine over 100 miles per day in an unsprung stage! No wonder people alit in San Francisco battered and bruised and swore never to ride another stage.

The two times I've slept in the park, the place was deserted. However, the ranger warned me that on Easter or other big weekends, the park fills up. Most sites are first come, first served, so plan to arrive early. The rest of the time, Vallecito is a welcome drop-in relief from the other organized campgrounds in the area, such as Borrego Palm Canyon and Tamarisk Grove.

Nearby hiking is available. You can bushwhack in the desert across the road or trek up the sandy wash of Smuggler Canyon. A short car ride away, you'll find Emigrant Trail and Blair Valley to the north, and trailheads at Bow Willow in the south. A good gem-hunting trip is located south, on S-2 almost to Ocotillo. On the left is Shell Canyon Road. Drive as far as you can, then hike. The canyon is filled with fossil shells and onyx. Go east on S-80 4 miles past Ocotillo and turn left on Painted Gorge Road. Again, be careful of the sand. There are agate and jasper immediately on the left and fossils in the hills to the right farther up the mountain. This is a good hike even if you aren't interested in gems.

To get there: from L.A., take I-10 east to I-15. Go south to Temecula. Take CA 79 east to Julian and CA 78 down Banner Grade to Scissors Crossing. Then take S-2 about 18 miles to the park.

KEY INFORMATION

Vallecito Regional Park
Department of Parks and Recreation
5201 Ruffin Road, Suite P
San Diego, CA 92123-1699

Operated by: County of San Diego

Information: (858) 694-3049; www.co.san-diego.ca.us/cnty/cntydepts/landuse/parks/camping

Open: June to September

Individual sites: 22 for RVs, trailers, and tents; 21 for tents only

Each site has: Picnic table, barbecue, fireplace

Registration: By entrance; for caravan and youth area reservations call (858) 565-3600

Facilities: Water, flush toilets, playground

Parking: At individual sites

Fee: $8

Elevation: 1,500 feet

Restrictions:

Pets—On 6-foot or shorter leash only; must be attended at all times; $1 fee

Fires—In established barbecue stoves or fire rings

Vehicles—RVs or trailers

Other—No generators

THE DESERT

WHITE TANK CAMPGROUND

Joshua Tree National Park

W hy is the arborescent tree yucca (*Yucca brevifolia*) called the Joshua tree? I have it on good authority that a group of Mormons were laboring across the trackless wastes, under a blazing sun, when they entered a *Yucca brevifolia* forest. Out of nowhere a cloud blocked the sun. In their ecstasy, the pioneers proclaimed the strange plants Joshua trees, referencing the Old Testament prophet who called on God block the sun. Indeed, the tufted branches resemble an old, robed prophet imploring the heavens with raised hands.

I visited Joshua Tree National Park with a group of friends. We taxed our bones trekking up the strenuous trail to the top of Ryan Mountain. When my wife, who stopped speaking to me on the rigorous ascent, saw the snows on Mount San Jacinto and the Little San Bernardinos and the Lost Horse Valley spread below, she relented graciously and acknowledged that the carrot was worth the climb.

Then came White Tank Campground, where we found a cozy campsite in an alcove in the rocks. The pitch was soft and sandy, and boulders blocked the wind. We packed a lunch basket and set out to find White Tank using the following instructions: "Take the Arch Rock Trail. When you come to the sign that designates 'Arch,' stop and look around. To the south, 20 feet away, see the slabs of sandwiched rock. Climb over those keeping the Arch

CAMPGROUND RATINGS

Beauty: ★★★★★
Site privacy: ★★★
Site spaciousness: ★★★
Quiet: ★★★★
Security: ★★★★
Cleanliness/upkeep: ★★★★

Don't get caught alive here in the summer! Otherwise, White Tank has incredibly beautiful, dramatic winter and spring camping.

Rock on the left, and you'll come down into sandy sheltered White Tank, a prime place for a picnic." Indeed we did, and with minimal difficulty. We learned to slide down the steep rocks on our bottoms. The quartz monzonite boulders found here stick tight to blue jeans and sneakers, simlifying an otherwise hairy climb.

White Tank lived up to its billing. It was warm in the sun and cool under the huge rocks, and the sand was as white and clean as a Bahama beach. What a lunch!

Afterward, we backtracked to the "Arch" sign. Somewhere out there was Grand Tank, a body of water with colonies of fairy and tadpole shrimp. How did they get here? The friendly ranger at the Park H.Q. in 29 Palms told me their ancestors hitched a ride to Grand Tank on the feet of migrating ducks!

To find Grand Tank, head downhill from the "Arch" sign and follow the trail that goes across a wash and up a hill. After a bit, the trail splits. We went left. "Follow the strong trail!" I urged my companions, who suggested I engrave that on my tombstone when we reached a dead end. Backing up, we climbed west to find the "strong trail" again. We saw birds diving into what we discovered were Grand Tank and the stream running south from it.

Vindicated at last, I identified white-winged doves and house finches circling the water. Grand Tank is about 15 feet deep. I looked in vain for the much-vaunted, hitchhiking shrimp. As the day went on, I led my group of doubting Thomases south along the stream and safely back to camp.

That night there was a full moon. With field glasses we examined the figure on the lunar surface to see if it was indeed a long-eared rabbit as the Chinese believe or, in fact, the man widely pub-licized in my youth. Swayed perhaps because the next day was Easter, I con-ceded that it might be a rabbit after all.

A mile and a half back toward the Park H.Q. in 29 Palms is Belle Campground, just as charming as White Tank and as accessible to the California Riding and Hiking Trail. The trail, which crosses Cot-tonwood Springs Road between the two campgrounds, is best in early-morning and evening, when twilight gives the flat desert rich hues and texture. Along with Ryan Campground in Lost Horse Valley, Belle and White Tank offer the best camp-ing in Joshua Tree. Other campgrounds are overrun by RVs and rock climbers in fall and spring—the only time you want to be caught alive in this desert.

It's not a bad idea to check the weather report before you come to Joshua Tree. The wind comes as Santa Anas in the fall and from the coast in the winter bringing rain. When it really blows, you must de-cide whether to tie your tent to the car or actually get into the car. Sometimes it will blow for days—sometimes hours.

In any season, you can dine at the wonderfully idiosyncratic 29 Palms Inn adjacent to the Park H.Q. on the Oasis of Mara, 29 Palm's original raison d'être. Walk around and look at the ducks on the pond, the beautiful truck garden fenced by palm fronds, and guest cabins that once belonged to miners.

KEY INFORMATION

**White Tank Campground
Joshua Tree National Park
74485 National Park Drive
29 Palms, CA 92277**

Operated by: National Park Service

Information: (760) 367-5522; www.nps.gov/jotr

Open: All year

Individual sites: 15

Each site has: Picnic table, fire ring

Registration: Not required

Facilities: Pit toilets, bring plenty of water

Parking: At site

Fee: None

Elevation: 3,800 feet

Restrictions:

Pets—On leash only

Fires—In fireplaces (bring your own firewood or charcoal)

Vehicles—RVs up to 27 feet

Other—All vegetation in park protected; limit of 6 people, 2 tents, and 2 vehicles per site

To get there: from L.A., take I-10 east to CA 62 past Banning over the San Gor-gonio Pass. Go north and east to 29 Palms. Drive 8 miles south on the Utah Trail to the intersection with Cottonwood Springs Road. Then go left (south) 1.5 miles to the camp-ground.

SOUTHERN CALIFORNIA

THE NORTHERN SIERRAS

ATWELL MILL CAMPGROUND

Mineral King, Sequoia National Park

Drive through torrid Visalia on any July afternoon and you'll know why the Yokut and Monache Native Americans fought over the summer camps by Atwell Mills, where it is pleasant during the day and cool at night. They built little round thatched houses and carpeted the floor with oak leaves and ferns. The women gathered most of the food, and the men spent most of their time in the sweat house telling lies. Summer was a time of plenty for them, with pine nuts, fish, manzanita cider, wild tobacco, and an occasional deer. The deer were stalked by one man alone in a deer disguise using arrows poisoned with rattle-snake venom. The Native Americans here led a great life, but it went like the wind when the white man appeared on the scene, hot after the riches of Mineral King.

The road up to Atwell Mill follows the old Native American trail. It's steep, but near Atwell Mill the ground levels out. This is one of the few areas around flat enough to camp and work on. A.J. Atwell of Visalia thought so as well and built a small sawmill in the meadow below the campground. You can still see the remains of the mill's steam engine near the stumps of the giant sequoias it helped reduce to shingles, grape stakes, and fence posts.

Steam engines tore their way through the American West. Anywhere there was fuel for the boiler, the engine could do the work of hundreds of men. Some Native Ameri-

CAMPGROUND RATINGS

Beauty: ★★★★★
Site privacy: ★★★★★
Site spaciousness: ★★★★★
Quiet: ★★★★
Security: ★★★★★
Cleanliness/upkeep: ★★★★★

Native Americans loved Atwell Mill, and so will you. This campground is one of the two best backcountry campgrounds in Sequoia National Park.

cans thought engines were a breed of devil, and, for them, I think that was true.

Folks knew how to build a steam engine for a thousand years before they could make iron durable enough for steam boilers. Finally, in England in 1600, a blacksmith experimented with burning coke in order to make a better frying pan and discovered the process that produces high-grade iron. That discovery ultimately enabled deforestation at Atwell Mill.

Still, there's a magic to

Atwell Mill. It's in the scarred stumps over a hundred years old. It's in the young sequoias reaching up in the shade of cedars, pines, and white firs. This is classic mountain camping.

All winter, the campsites are cleansed by 20 feet of snow. In the summer, the air smells clean and rich with the odor of redwood and pine. Walk up the little ridge above the campground and watch the sun set on the mountains across the Kaweah River. Or better yet, head down the Atwell Hockett Trail between campsites #16 and #17. The trail passes the supine steam engine on the right and heads over the hill. About 100 yards from the metal sign banning firearms and dogs, go to the right, about 30 yards down, to the famous Native American bathtubs. The rock outcropping there is a great place to have lunch or a sundowner. There, manzanita opens up the forest to give you a great view of the mountains and sky.

Back on the main trail, carry on past little Deadwood Creek to East Fork Kaweah River gorge with its giant sequoias and mist kicked up by the falls. Rough trails head up either side of the gorge for more private picnicking and sunning spots. Or, keep walking the many miles up to Hockett Meadows.

Another good hike is up the Atwell Redwood Trail. From the campground, walk back down the Mineral King Road you drove up on and find the trailhead at a curve about 500 yards down. Hike up the mountain into the Atwell Grove sequoias. Three of these trees are gigantic. At their feet are the bracken fern that the Native Americans used to carpet the floors of their houses. Keep hiking up and to the left along the ridge to Paradise Peak. The hike is about 9 miles round-trip and should take you all day.

Remember, when you leave Three Rivers you are bidding adieu to ice-and-beer country. The store at Silver King doesn't sell beer because of the dangerous road out, and their ice machine broke. So, ice up. Remember, block ice lasts about three days to cube ice's one.

The sign where the Mineral King Road takes off from CA 198 should tell you if Atwell Mills and Cold Springs have campsites available. However, this sign is not always up to date, so phone the Ranger Station up in Mineral King to make sure at (559) 565-3341. It *is* a three-hour round-trip, so you don't want to arrive and not find a campsite. On the Mineral King Road turn your lights on. It helps on-coming traffic see you a split second earlier, which means a lot on this hairy road. Bring bug repellent in August to deter biting pests. And, remember to use the bear boxes!

To get there: from L.A., take I-5 north over the Tejon Pass to CA 99. Drive north on CA 99 past Bakersfield. Take CA 65 north to Exeter. Go east (right) on CA 198 to Three Rivers. Three miles past Three Rivers turn right on the Mineral King Road. It's about 20 miles to Atwell Mill. Plan on the 20-mile trip taking 1.5 hours.

KEY INFORMATION

Atwell Mill Campground
Sequoia and Kings Canyon National Parks
47050 Generals Highway
Three Rivers, CA 93271-9651

Operated by: National Park Service

Information: (559) 565-3341; www.nps.gov/seki

Open: Memorial Day weekend to September (depending on road and weather conditions)

Individual sites: 21

Each site has: Picnic table, fire pits, bear boxes

Registration: At entrance

Facilities: Water, pit toilets

Parking: At site

Fee: $8

Elevation: 6,650 feet

Restrictions:

Pets—On leash only; not allowed on trails

Fires—Allowed in fireplaces

Vehicles—No RVs or trailers

Other—Don't leave food out; use bear boxes

BIG PINE CREEK CAMPGROUND

Big Pine Creek, Inyo National Forest

Eat breakfast in the town of Big Pine at the Country Kitchen where owners Jim and Liz serve up the morning special of one egg and a couple sausages in tandem with the tour de force—biscuits and gravy! I love biscuits and gravy, and so do all the cowpokes from miles around. This is real food. In the right belly at the right time, that gravy could write sonnets or fight wars. It's the fuel that won the West.

Camp at Big Pine Creek Campground, hike the surrounding trails, and sleep like the righteous. This campground is impossibly beautiful. Jump out of your tent in the morning to see the ice and snow on the Palisades, the southernmost active glacier in North America. The canyon walls are steep and gray and trimmed in light green. On the canyon floor Jeffrey pines shadow Big Pine Creek and the hopeful fishermen.

Big Pine Creek Campground is comfortable and suitable for a week's stay. The pit toilets are clean. The sites are mostly private and separated by trees. During my visit, the conscientious host ran around on his motorbike and policed empty campsites for cigarette butts, while the helpful hostess and her killer Scottie dog ran the show from the trailer. If you arrive and find Pine Creek Campground loaded, just head back down the road to Upper Sage Flat (21 sites) or Sage Flat (28 sites). Both are on the creek and almost as beautiful as Big Pine Creek Campground.

CAMPGROUND RATINGS

Beauty:	★★★★★
Site privacy:	★★★★★
Site spaciousness:	★★★★★
Quiet:	★★★
Security:	★★★★★
Cleanliness/upkeep:	★★★★★

Come to Big Pine Creek for good fishing, superb hiking, and leisurely camping.

In 1998, the nearby Glacier Lodge burned down. What remains is a small mini-mart where you can buy ice, beer, and sundries. You can also rent cabins from them. If you get tired of camp cooking, drive the easy 9 miles back to the town of Big Pine and eat at Rossi's Steak and Spaghetti. The Rossi family has lived nearby for generations, and mementos of their lives adorn the restaurant's walls.

Drive back up to Big Pine Campground and notice the large lateral moraines (ridges of dirt, gravel, and rock deposited by the glaciers). Note the U-shaped upper valley carved by glaciers in the ice ages. Cooler temperatures and heavy precipitation meant that winter snows didn't melt completely in the summer, so the snow fields grew larger and deeper until their weight turned old snow into glacial ice. Gravity tugged, and inevitably the glaciers became rivers of ice moving slowly downhill. They cut out steep cirques, stair-step lake basins, and, of course, U-shaped valleys. As the glaciers lumbered down, they picked up boulders and rocks along the way. This rubble was deposited when the glacier melted. Ridges of the debris, now moraines, formed along the edges and at the end point of the glacier. Glaciers of that size are all gone now. The Palisade Glacier above Big Pine Campground is a remnant from a mini ice age about 4,000 years ago.

Above the campground, the north and south forks of Big Pine Creek tumble down from the glaciers and flow together under the bridge in front of Glacier Lodge. The divided north and south canyons rise steeply from the lodge to the Sierra Crest. You can see Middle Palisade, Disappointment Peak, Clyde Peak, and Palisade Crest from here.

The walk leading to First Falls is fun and lasts about an hour, round-trip. Go across the bridge in front of the lodge and to the left up the road around the locked gate. Walk between the creek and private cabins on the right. Cross the bridge at the base of the falls and take the stone stairway to the right. Climb up through the woods to the old road (closed by an avalanche) and another wooden bridge. This is called Trail Camp. There are picnic tables and rest rooms. You can hike back down along the old road, crossing the south fork and winding past some cabins to the lodge.

For a longer hike, continue up the road above Trail Camp into a canyon to Second Falls. You can take either the signed Upper Trail or stay on the road leading to a steep trail on the right. Both come together above the Second Falls. This hike is about one-and-a-half additional hours round-trip from the First Falls.

Keep climbing above Second Falls and find screen actor Lon Chaney's cabin, built in 1925. This shady, creekside spot is a good place to picnic. More ambitious hikers can head for Brainard Lake, Willow Lake, and the Finger Lakes toward Sierra Crest or First through Seventh Lakes in the other direction. On all hikes, remember, you're up there at 7,700 feet and above. It's very dry. Drink water before you're thirsty.

KEY INFORMATION

Big Pine Creek Campground, Inyo National Forest

White Mountain Ranger Station
798 North Main Street
Bishop, CA 93514

Operated by: U.S. Forest Service

Information: (760) 873-2500; www.r5.fs.fed.us/inyo

Open: May to mid-October

Individual sites: 30

Each site has: Picnic table, barbeque grill

Registration: At entrance; reserve by phone, (877) 444-6777, or online, www.reserveUSA.com

Facilities: Water, pit toilets

Parking: At site

Fee: $11; $8.65 nonrefundable reservation fee

Elevation: 7,700 feet

Restrictions:

Pets—On leash only

Fires—In fireplace

Vehicles—No limit

To get there: from L.A., take I-5 north to CA 14. Go north to U.S. 395 near Inyokern. Continue north on U.S. 395 for 108 miles to the town of Big Pine. From Big Pine, drive west on Glacier Lodge Road 9 miles to the lodge and Big Pine Creek Campground.

BUCKEYE FLAT CAMPGROUND

Giant Forest Village, Sequoia National Park

Buckeye Flat is a good sleeping camp-ground. The sun rises over the mountains behind you, allowing for good snoozing until about 10 A.M. The rushing cataract of the Middle Fork of the Kaweah River supplies comforting white noise. And, with only tent camping allowed, you won't awake to a morning TV show or humming generator from a nearby RV.

Then, you crawl out of the mummy bag into a beautiful world. Morning mists swirl about the high peaks and green slopes. Peer down at the Kaweah River and see a gorge out of the movie *Last of the Mohicans*. Walk the narrow campground access road, and even that is beautiful. Paralleling the gorge, it was built by the Civilian Conservation Corps in the 1930s, when men could still work with rock.

In May, when the buckeyes, or horse chestnuts, around the campground bloom, they seem tipped with pom-poms. By late August, the leaves fall, and the trees show the pear-like seed pods hanging from their bare branches. The Native Americans used buckeye meat in much the same way they did that of acorns—by repeatedly leaching and drying the meal until edible. It was also used as a fish poison. Apparently, a mash of buckeyes thrown into a small stream would stupify the fish, so they would float to the surface and be taken by nets.

Don't expect to see any sequoias around Buckeye Campground. The park's sequoias

CAMPGROUND RATINGS

Beauty: ★★★★★
Site privacy: ★★★
Site spaciousness: ★★★
Quiet: ★★★★★
Security: ★★★★★
Cleanliness/upkeep: ★★★★★

Buckeye Flat Campground, like a scene out of Last of the Mohicans, *is by a magical gorge.*

are up much higher—above 5,000 feet. The sequoia is the earth's largest living tree. (Termites compose the earth's largest biomass, however!) The tree reproduces from seeds the size of an oatmeal flake. Imagine.

Once growing all over the western United States—even as far south as the Santa Monica Mountains—the *Sequoiadendron giganteum* retreated to 70 groves on the western slope of the Sierra when, after the last ice age, the climate grew too dry for the moisture-loving trees.

Used only for fence posts and shingles, the huge sequoias (possibly named after a Native American, Sequoyah, who established an alphabet for the Cherokee language) were threatened by loggers in the jolly days of the West when anything that was big had to fall. "God has cared for these trees...but He cannot save them from fools. Only Uncle Sam can do that" (John Muir). Thank God, Uncle Sam did, in 1890, by establishing Sequoia National Park.

Buckeye Flat offers good spring camping. Bring chains for your tires if you want to drive up Generals Highway to see the big trees, because it snows here even in late spring. Rangers will stop you and turn you around if you don't have the required chains when it is snowing up top.

Plan to visit when the campground opens in April and you can combine cross-country skiing in the mountains with camping and wildflowers lower down. (Buckeye has an elevation of 2,800 feet.) There are places to rent skis and marked trails in Lodgepole. Buy the *Wildflowers* book at a park visitors center and see how many you can identify. At the beginning of May, we saw yucca, buttercup, milkweed, sunflowers, purple lupine, and ceanothus (wild lilac), as well as the white flowers of the buckeye.

The first thing you'll notice about the campsites at Buckeye are the steel bear boxes. Use them! Keep your food in them at all times. There is water, but it's heavily chlorinated, so bring drinking water. The flush-toilet bathrooms are spare and spotless. Considering that the campground is on a mountainside, there are good flat places on each site to pitch tents. Don't forget to take the trail just south of the campground that goes along Paradise Creek.

Be aware of the weather. Phone ahead and talk to the rangers. Make sure Buckeye Flat is open. Rangers have, in the past, closed the campground because of temporarily troublesome bears breaking into cars. Buy last minute stuff at Three Rivers. This charming little town has just about everything you could need.

A great drive on the way out is down Yokohl Drive through the Yokohl Valley to Springville. This is old California—a thin strip of asphalt running along the Yokohl through cattle country. This was the trail the mule teams followed coming from San Francisco to supply the Cerro Gordo mine over the Sierras in the Owens Valley. There were water and grass for the mules. And, the native grass in those days was green year-round. So much for the golden hills of California, which arrived only with the competing European seasonal grasses brought in by early ranchers.

To get there: from L.A., take I-5 north over the Tejon Pass to CA 99. Drive north on CA 99 past Bakersfield. Take CA 65 north to Exeter. Go east (right) on CA 198 to Three Rivers. Continue to the CA 198 entrance to Sequoia National Park. Drive 6 miles into the park and take the signed mile-long road on the right to the campground.

KEY INFORMATION

**Buckeye Flat Campground
Sequoia and Kings Canyon
National Parks
47050 Generals Highway
Three Rivers, CA 93271**

Operated by: National Park Service

Information: (559) 565-3341; www.nps.gov/seki California Road Conditions (CALTRANS), (800) 427-7673

Open: April to October (depending on road and weather conditions)

Individual sites: 28

Each site has: Picnic table, fire pit, bear box

Registration: At entrance

Facilities: Water, flush toilets

Parking: At site

Fee: $14

Elevation: 2,800 feet

Restrictions:

Pets—On leash only; not allowed on trails

Fires—In fire pits

Vehicles—No RVs or trailers

Other—Keep food in bear boxes, not in tents or cars

THE NORTHERN SIERRAS

COLD SPRINGS CAMPGROUND

Mineral King, Sequoia National Park

Cold Springs Campground is the most beautiful campground in Southern California. Down by the gorgeous Kaweah River, this campground is situated in the shadows of Sawtooth and Mineral Peaks, Needham and Rainbow Mountains, and to the south, Miners Ridge. Winter scours out the valley so it feels brand new every summer. A cataract cuts through the walk-in camping area. The rush of the water is white noise; you'll sleep like a baby. I love this campground.

Back in the 1870s, miners took one look at the rocks in Mineral King and rushed in. What excited them was the contact zone between reddish metamorphics and grayish granite. So sure of silver was Thomas Fowler, a wealthy rancher from Tulare County, that he bet his entire fortune on his Empire Mine, boasting that he would pay off America's national debt and then buy Ireland to free it from the tyrannical British. First, Fowler built the road into Mineral King. A local reporter described the mine's opening: "I doubt that General Grant felt more proud when he rode into Richmond than did honest Tom Fowler when he rode into Mineral King..."

Of course, the mine went bust. Avalanches swept away the mine, the town, and the mile-long bucket tramway to the stamp mill in the valley. All that was left of Fowler's dream was the road, and folks used it to get away from the brutal heat in

CAMPGROUND RATINGS

Beauty:	★★★★★
Site privacy:	★★★★★
Site spaciousness:	★★★★★
Quiet:	★★★★★
Security:	★★★★★
Cleanliness/upkeep:	★★★★★

This is the most beautiful campground in the adjacent Sequoia and Kings Canyon National Parks. Check on available space before driving up Mineral King Road—it's a bear!

---

the Central Valley below. In 1893, the federal government declared the area part of the Sierra Forest Preserve.

In the 1960s, the Forest Service considered building a major ski resort at Mineral King. The Walt Disney Corporation proposed a resort with a skiing capacity of 10,000 persons daily. Widespread opposition and law suits from environmental groups ensued, and finally, in 1978, Congress made Mineral King part of Sequoia National Park.

Now Mineral King is famous for its marmots. These little devils have a penchant for gnawing on auto parts from early spring to about mid-July. They chew on hoses, fan belts, and electrical wiring. Some people bring chicken wire to put around their cars. Unless you park on a hard surface and seal the edges of the wire with piled rocks, so the marmots can't dig their way in, the chicken wire just makes a big marmot playpen. In springtime, leave your car in the hikers' parking lot in Atwell Mill Campground, and get a lift up to Mineral King. As the summer progresses, the chewing ends, and marmot-safe parking reaches higher altitudes until it is safe to park at the trailheads in Mineral King. It's a good idea to phone the rangers and ask about the latest on marmot activity. You don't want to pay $250 to get towed to Three Rivers.

Don't hate the humble marmot. It's a brave little rodent. With hair standing on end and long claws at the ready, the feisty marmot clatters his sharp teeth and whistles loudly at enemies. Marmots are superbly created to survive in a harsh environment. Their bodies afford "clear and cogent arguments of the wisdom and design of the Author" (Robert Boyle, 1688). And, it's against federal law to use poison or other substances to kill, deter, or otherwise foil marmots from car-gnawing.

Remember to get supplies in Three Rivers. Put drinks in a gunny sack and store them in the Kaweah River. That'll chill the cans.

Think about using the walk-in campsites at Cold Springs, nestled in a corner between the Kaweah River and a cataract that pours down to the river. To access the walk-ins, take the second right loop and follow it to the parking lot at the end. Bring rucksacks to carry your stuff the hundred yards or so into the sites. There is piped water and a pit toilet in among the sites.

A trail (3 miles round-trip) heading east from Cold Springs Campground (trailhead between sites #6 and #7) directs you along a signed nature trail. I found out that corn lilies are also called skunk cabbage and that juniper seeds need to be partially digested by birds in order to sprout, which means they grow far away from their parent trees. Stay on the trail, which hits a road to the right of Mineral King Village and arrives at the trailhead for Tufa Falls (another easy hike) and other destinations heading up Farewell Canyon.

Plan on spending more than a day or so in Mineral King. You could spend most of the summer hiking out of Cold Springs Campground, but give yourself a day or two to get used to the altitude.

To get there: from L.A., take I-5 north over the Tejon Pass to CA 99. Drive north on CA 99 past Bakersfield. Take CA 65 north to Exeter. Go east (right) on CA 198 to Three Rivers. Three miles past Three Rivers turn right onto Mineral King Road. It's about 25 miles to Cold Springs Campground. Plan on the 25-mile trip taking 1.5 hours.

KEY INFORMATION

Cold Springs Campground
Sequoia and Kings Canyon National Parks
47050 Generals Highway
Three Rivers, CA 93271-9651

Operated by: National Park Service

Information: (559) 565-3341; www.nps.gov/seki

Open: Memorial Day weekend to September (depending on road and weather conditions)

Individual sites: 40

Each site has: Picnic table, fire pit, bear box

Registration: At entrance

Facilities: Water, pit toilets

Parking: At site

Fee: $8

Elevation: 7,500 feet

Restrictions:

Pets—On leash only; not allowed on trails

Fires—Allowed in fire pits

Vehicles—No RVs or trailers

Other—No marmot molesting; keep food in bear boxes, not in tents or cars

DORST CAMPGROUND

Giant Forest Village, Sequoia National Park

Dorst Campground is about family. On arrival you'll notice squads of children splashing in the nonthreatening Dorst Creek or racing up and down the grassy slopes, as well as moms pushing their infants around in strollers. Most of the folks are tent campers laagered together in the tent-only loops, and their children quickly become friends. I saw lots of dads relaxing in aluminum lawn chairs, free and happy.

On the Generals Highway, Dorst is a perfect base camp from which to explore Giant Forest, Grant Grove, and, farther afield, Cedar Grove. Not too far away is Hume Lake with big-time swimming prospects. A quick run will get you groceries or grits at Lodgepole or Stony Creek Lodge.

An early explorer of what is now Sequoia National Park, William Brewer, wrote: "Such a landscape! A hundred peaks in sight over thirteen thousand feet—many very sharp, deep canyons, cliffs in every direction almost rivaling Yosemite, sharp ridges almost inaccessible to man, on which human foot has never trod—all combined to produce a view the subliminity of which is rarely equal, one which few are privileged to behold."

The Park Service has fought hard to keep it that way. In fact, one of their biggest fights was against sheep. The mountains were perfect for sheepherding. The sheep ran amok through the forests eating every-

CAMPGROUND RATINGS

Beauty:	★★★★
Site privacy:	★★★
Site spaciousness:	★★★★
Quiet:	★★★★
Security:	★★★★
Cleanliness/upkeep:	★★★★★

Dorst Campground is a good summer family campground with wonderful side trips. Stay at least three days.

thing in sight, ripping it all up by the roots. Kings Canyon was fast becoming a high-altitude desert. The park superintendent called out the U.S. Cavalry, and still the sheep and sheepherds kept coming. Only when the superintendent hit on the strategy of banning sheep on one side of the Sierras and sheepherds on the other side was the ovine feeding frenzy discouraged.

A great hike from Dorst Campground leads to the Muir Grove of giant sequoias. Even if you poke along, the round-trip shouldn't take more than four hours. Find the trailhead at the Dorst Campground amphitheater (follow the beehive symbol west). The trail is signed and leads you up through white firs and sugar pines, then over a ridge to the Muir Grove giants. The good news is that the return trip is mostly downhill.

Another nearby hike is up Little Baldy. The trailhead is 1.6 miles south of the Dorst Campground entrance on Generals Highway. Park in the pull-off area at the Little Baldy Saddle and head northeast. Two hard miles later you're on the bare granite Little Baldy summit. It's not a great place to be in a thunderstorm, but it's fine for lying in the noon sun.

If you tire of Dorst Campground family fun, or if you arrive and the campground is full, an alternative lies in the neighboring Sierra National Forest. Leave Dorst Campground and turn left up Generals Highway toward Grant Grove. Turn right on Big Meadow Road and drive about 5 miles to Big Meadows Campground Number 3. Pass up the heavily used Big Meadows Campground Numbers 1 and 2. Below Number 3, Boulder Creek spills down rocky chutes and gathers in pools. There is good dipping there, but be careful. The rock is slippery.

Or, pick up a fire permit as you pass the Hume Lake Forest Service Station on CA 180, and you can camp in one of literally thousands of wonderful potential sites for hunkering down overnight.

Further down the white knuckle Big Meadow Road is Horse Corral Meadow, where, in 1922, a cowpoke named Jessie Agnew killed the last grizzly bear in California, claiming it was after his cattle. Imagine, killing the last California grizzly, our state animal!

Back at Big Meadows Campground, look for a brown, fiberglass post marking a trailhead. From here, you can hike up to Weaver Lake or Jennie Lake. Take the trail about 2 miles to Fox Meadow where there's a small wooden sign and a trail register. Weaver Lake is straight ahead about 1.5 miles. The trail to Jennie Lake, to the right, heads south 5 miles.

The best way into Dorst Campground is up CA 180 from Fresno. The other road in, through Three Rivers, is a bear. It's narrow, slow, and scary. When you arrive at Dorst Campground, check out all the loops. I camped in a loop allowing trailers and found the campsite much roomier and more private than the sites on the tent-only loops.

Try to camp at Dorst long enough to relax and get to know the area. I think three days is a minimum. One day just doesn't get it. Camping has its own clock, and it runs slowly.

To get there: from L.A., take I-5 north over the Tejon Pass to CA 99. Drive north on CA 99 to Fresno. Turn right on CA 198 and drive to Kings Canyon National Park. Turn right (south) on Generals Highway and drive 16 miles to Dorst Campground on the right.

KEY INFORMATION

Dorst Campground
Sequoia and Kings Canyon National Parks
47050 Generals Highway
Three Rivers, CA 93271-9651

Operated by: National Park Service

Information: (559) 565-3341; www.nps.gov/seki

Open: June to September (depending on road and snow conditions)

Individual sites: 219

Each site has: Picnic table, fire pits, bear boxes

Registration: At entrance; reserve by phone, (800) 365-2267, or online, www.reservations.nps.gov

Facilities: Water, flush toilets

Parking: At site

Fee: $16

Elevation: 6,700 feet

Restrictions:

Pets—On leash only

Fires—In fire pits

Vehicles—No limits

Other—Keep food in bear boxes, not in tents or cars

EAST FORK CAMPGROUND

Rock Creek Lake, Inyo National Forest

D riving from Los Angeles to East Fork, you'll go through Mojave, the desert, and then the Owens Valley, a *graben* according to geologists, which means it's a 100-mile-long, 5-mile-wide trench between the Sierras on the west and the White-Inyo Mountains on the east. It's a magical place, and the Native Americans coined the name *Inyo,* meaning "dwelling place of the great spirit."

It is a land of dramatic contrast and incredible beauty, where mountain and desert meld into breathtaking scenery and glaciered peaks tower over shimmering alkali flats. Tumbling mountain streams become lost in the desert, and gem-like lakes shimmer against deep pine forests.

East Fork Campground on Rock Creek lies right in the heart of the beast. Rock Creek is in a glacial cirque (basin) and drops 6,000 feet and 20 miles to the Owens River. On the way to East Fork, you'll pass Bishop (the last good town for shopping); don't forget to stop at Mahogany Smoked Meats on U.S. 395 as you leave town. Buy some smoked pork chops for that night's dinner. Gnaw on some world-famous slab jerky as you drive up the infamous Sherwin Grade (or Vaporlock Grade as the old-timers called it). You'll climb 24 miles and about 3,000 feet to Tom's Place, where you will turn south on Rock Creek Road.

Stop at Tom's Place. It's a restaurant/ store/bar/cabin complex where you can

CAMPGROUND RATINGS

Beauty: ★★★★★
Site privacy: ★★★★★
Site spaciousness: ★★★
Quiet: ★★★
Security: ★★★★★
Cleanliness/upkeep: ★★★★★

Some say Rock Creek features the best camping in the Sierras. Don't forget the beef jerky in Bishop and the gut-plug pancakes at Tom's Place.

get fishing information and the bait the trout are hitting that day. You can buy last-minute camping supplies or eat some of the gut-plug pancakes for breakfast or gravy-soaked chicken fried steak for dinner.

Head up Rock Creek Road. Pass French Camp Campground. It's a lovely campground by the creek. It's almost 1,500 feet lower than East Fork Campground, which makes it a good place to camp in the spring, when the flowers are out down below and East Fork is still socked in with winter cold. At East Fork Campground the bloom arrives later in the summer.

As Owens Valley writer Mary Austin observed, "Well up from the valley, at the confluence of canyons, are delectable summer meadows. Fireweed flames about them against gray boulders; streams are open, go smoothly about the glacier slips and make deep bluish pools for trout. Pines raise statelier shafts and give themselves room to grow gentians, shinleaf, and little grass of Parnassus in their golden checkered shadows; the meadow is white with violets and all outdoors keeps the clock."

Find the entrance to East Fork Campground at about 9,000 feet (Pep Boys sells a car altimeter for less than $20, which is surprisingly accurate and fun to watch). The campground is down on Rock Creek. Most of the sites on the creek are lovely, but in the open, and have RV-size parking spots. Other sites, back up from the creek, are small and private. The parking spots are half a dozen yards from the campsites, which are mostly private and secluded in little copses of pine, brush, and aspen.

When I was there in late September, the aspen leaves were turning gold. When the wind blew they shimmered so prettily in the sunlight and made a soft, tinny clatter as they shook. The creek was well stocked. Happy fishermen tromped back to their campfires with strings of nice-sized trout for dinner. At night, the cold snapped, and, in the morning, our camping neighbors all exclaimed how nippy it was.

The hardy ridges above the riparian campground are covered with isolated foxtail pines. The creek goes north and south, so the sun is quick to set at night and slow to rise in the morning. At 9,000 feet, you really want the sun and will walk with your morning coffee to find it. A good evening walk is across the bridges to the other side of the creek. Go to site #108, the host's site, and across the access road, you'll find the first bridge. There is fine fishing here.

A good hike is up the creek to Rock Creek Lake. The trail leaves on the north side of the campground by site #82 and goes all the way to Rock Creek Lake, passing some small campgrounds and a resort before hitting the lake and trailheads to the high country.

Above Rock Creek Lake, you'll find Mosquito Flat. You can drive there and park at 10,250 feet. From there, it's an easy day hike into the John Muir Wilderness and Little Lakes Valley. The valley is a pretty glacial trough below 13,000-foot peaks. Bring your wildflower book because the meadows up there are loaded with them.

To get there: from L.A., take I-5 north to CA 14. Go north to U.S. 395 near Inyokern. Continue north on U.S. 395 to Bishop. From Bishop, drive 24 miles north on U.S. 395 and exit to the west at Tom's Place onto Rock Creek Road. Drive 5 miles up Rock Creek Road to the campground.

KEY INFORMATION

East Fork Campground
Inyo National Forest
873 North Main Street
Bishop, CA 93514

Operated by: U.S. Forest Service

Information: (760) 873-2500; www.r5.fs.fed.us/inyo

Open: May to November

Individual sites: 133

Each site has: Picnic table, fireplace

Registration: At entrance; reserve by phone, (877) 444-6777, or online, www.reserveUSA.com

Facilities: Water, flush toilets

Parking: At site

Fee: $12; $8.65 nonrefundable reservation fee.

Elevation: 9,000 feet

Restrictions:

Pets—Allowed

Fires—In fireplace

Vehicles—RVs up to 22 feet

FAIRVIEW CAMPGROUND

Fairview, Sequoia National Forest

A bout 60,000 years ago, a glacier flowing down an earthquake slip fault cut the U-shaped Upper Kern Canyon. Look southward along the Upper Kern Canyon and you can see how the glacier carved out the canyon, giving it rounded shoulders. In the Lower Kern Canyon, below Lake Isabella where the glacier didn't flow, the shoulders of the canyon are sharp and V-shaped.

Fairview Campground, near the head of the Upper Kern Valley, is the best camping spot in the area. It's set down by the river, well below the road and any traffic noise, with the mountains towering around. The sites are so well planned, it's hard to decide where to camp. The last time I was there it was spring, and the snow level was down to 5,000 feet, but it was warm and sunny down in the campground.

All the flowers were out—most ostentatiously the purple yerba santa. We made a tea out of its leaves, which the Native Americans thought was good for coughs, colds, asthma, and the like. Pretty bitter stuff. I've also heard that the leaves, when pounded into a poultice, cure sores. The Spanish used the leaves as tobacco, for chewing and smoking. Others claim that you can chew the leaves to quench thirst. After the first bitter taste subsides, you'll feel a sweet, cooling sensation. I tried it, and it wasn't too bad.

CAMPGROUND RATINGS

Beauty: ★★★★★
Site privacy: ★★★★
Site spaciousness: ★★★★
Quiet: ★★★★
Security: ★★★★
Cleanliness/upkeep: ★★★★

Fairview Campground offers the best tent camping in the Lake Isabella area. Be careful with children around the river. Don't miss McNally's "we-grind-our-own-meat" cheeseburgers.

'By our campsite, we found a flowering flannel bush (*Fremontia californica*) with brazen yellow flowers bright against the white water of the Kern. All night, the strong current rattled the rocks on the river bottom. In the morning, the ranger, who came by to collect our $12, admired our flannel bush and reported that the bark can be brewed and gargled to relieve a sore throat.

Fairview has always been blessed. The Native Americans used it as a fall and spring campground. In the

late 1800s, Stony Rhymes and Lucien Barbeau had a cow camp on the bend of the river. In 1910, Matt and Lupie Burlando moved to Fairview and built the Fairview Lodge. They rented rooms to tourists who came for fishing and hunting. Matt built a swinging bridge (you can still see it today) across the river to the natural hot springs on the west side and ran packing trips into the backcountry. After Matt and Lupie's children reached school age, the entire family moved down to Kernville to be near the school. Fairview went back to being a cow camp for a while before Johnny McNally opened McNally's Steakhouse. Johnny was an amazing rodeo rider and a deputy sheriff, and his wife, Pauline, could shoot a running buck with a rifle from the back of a galloping horse.

To reach McNally's from the campground, walk south along the river 50 yards. You'll find McNally's Steakhouse, the hamburger hut, and the gas station/grocery store. We loaded up on beer, hot dogs, and ice at the store and then hunkered down at the outside picnic tables for some rousing chili burgers before heading across the suspension bridge on a diet-redeeming hike along

Flynn Trail. (See the map and handout sheet on the display by the parking lot near the hamburger stand.) You'll find access here for the Tobias Trail as well. Maybe the best short day hikes here are on the Whiskey Flat Trail, which runs from the bridge down to the north end of Burlando Road in Kernville. The trail parallels the west side of the river and runs through high chaparral, digger pines, and oak. There are wonderful places along the trail for picnicking. Put down a blanket and snooze while the river runs below you. I've heard there's good fishing here. Another good hike is up the trail to Salmon Creek Falls. The marked trailhead is a mile or so south of Fairview to the east.

One word of warning about the Kern River. It is very dangerous. When I was last there in May, it was running way above its natural banks. Camping there with children is only advisable if they are sternly warned and constantly watched. The water is cold, and the current is strong. If you're camping with children, go down below on Lake Isabella. I especially recommend Tillie Creek Campground, which is pretty, safe, and flat. Bring the children's bicycles. There is even a playground. In the spring, good fishing can be found in the lake as well.

KEY INFORMATION

**Fairview Campground,
Sequoia National Forest
Greenhorn District
P.O. Box 3810
Lake Isabella, CA 92340**

Operated by: U.S. Forest Service

Information: (760) 379-5646; www.r5.fs.fed.us/sequoia

Open: April to November

Individual sites: 55

Each site has: Fire ring, picnic table

Registration: Host will collect on rounds; reserve by phone, (877) 444-6777, or online, www.reserveUSA.com

Facilities: Water, vault toilets

Parking: At site

Fee: $12; $14 on holiday weekends; $5 for each additional vehicle

Elevation: 3,500 feet

Restrictions:

Pets—On leash only

Fires—In fireplaces

Vehicles—RVs up to 45 feet

To get there: from L.A., take I-5 north over the Tejon Pass to CA 99. Drive north on CA 99 past Bakersfield. Take CA 178 east to Lake Isabella. Take CA 155 north to Wofford Heights. Bear right to Kernville. From Kernville, drive north 16 miles on Kern River Highway–Sierra Road to Fairview Campground on the left.

FOUR JEFFREY CAMPGROUND / SABRINA CAMPGROUND

Lake Sabrina, Inyo National Forest

The princess of campgrounds on Bishop Creek above Bishop is tiny Sabrina Campground perched on the lip of Lake Sabrina. At 9,000 feet, the view of the picture-perfect lake, the glaciered mountain peaks marbled with rusty red metamorphic rock, and the deep blue sky is breathtaking. Sit on the sunny patio of the Lake Sabrina Boat Landing and eat an incredible old-fashioned hamburger grilled up by the pleasant hostess. That's how you know you're not in Switzerland after all, but in the Wild West.

You'll see lanky anglers swigging Bud, a big husky dog asleep atop an up-turned aluminum boat, and cowpokes in ten-gallon hats stepping out of canoes, holding up six-pound trout, just caught, their bright colors catching the sun. Then, oddly, a pack train of laden llamas will file up the trail across the lake. Llamas? In the Wild West? Yes, apparently some of the local pack outfits use llamas. Indigenous to Peruvian high country, the llamas take to the Sierras like ducks to water.

Drive the vertiginous, short dirt road up to North Lake and check out North Lake Campground at the trailhead. No trailers, no RVs, only tents, but like Sabrina Campground and most of the campgrounds in the Bishop Creek area, it has few sites. The only campground around that has enough space to be a destination campground is Four Jeffrey, which is down the road from

CAMPGROUND RATINGS

Beauty:	★★★★
Site privacy:	★★★★
Site spaciousness:	★★★★★
Quiet:	★★★★★
Security:	★★★★★
Cleanliness/upkeep:	★★★★★

Four Jeffrey Campground is the best destination campground in the Bishop Creek Drainage area. Later, try to find a spot in Sabrina Campground.

Sabrina Lake and to the right, on the spur road to South Lake.

Four Jeffrey is an impressive campground. The surrounding mountains are spare and dry, and the view is incredible—although not eye-popping stunning like the views from Sabrina and North Lake. The South Fork of Bishop Creek runs through the campground. Many of the sites are down by the water, which is alive with trout. Others are up the hill in low brush. This area makes for good spring and

early-summer camping. By fall, the hillside is muted and austere. I like that look, but others want the green of the pines.

Make Four Jeffrey the first-night destination campground in the Bishop Creek area. Chances of getting a site there are very good (the camping season at Four Jeffrey is two months longer than at Sabrina Campground). The next day, cruise around. Hit Sabrina Campground first, then North Lake Campground, then the other little campgrounds up and down the forks of Bishop Creek and see if you find something you like better.

It was at Four Jeffrey Campground that I thrilled to the efficacy of the cool, semi-new miner's lights sold in the camping stores. Ranging from cheap to pretty expensive, these babies are cinched around your head, so the light is on your forehead and the beam follows your eyes. My wife lost her contact lens somewhere around camp, and I went scouting for it. The light was better than ten camp lanterns. I found the lost lens with ease. Buy one of these lights. The more expensive ones are more comfortable, but the batteries and bulbs may be more difficult to purchase.

Part of my attraction to Four Jeffrey Campground has to do with survival. All the other campgrounds except little North Lake are by the streambed. And, the Bishop area is earthquake country. At 2:30 A.M. in March of 1872, a monster quake hit the Owens Valley. It was felt as far east as Salt Lake City, as far north as Canada, and as far south as Mexico. It shook old John Muir over in Yosemite Valley. He described the incident: "I was awakened by a tremendous earthquake, and though I had never enjoyed a storm of this sort, the strange thrilling motion could not be mistaken, and I ran out of cabin, both glad and frightened, shouting, 'A noble earthquake! A noble earthquake!' feeling sure I was going to learn something."

John Muir used to strap himself in the tops of pine trees during thunderstorms. He was lucky. Well, the 27 folks down in Lone Pine who died in the 1872 quake weren't so lucky. I figure a quake like that could happen again, and the dams up on Sabrina and South Lake would go pretty easily. I want to be sleeping on the high ground at Four Jeffrey Campground, so I can snooze right through the flood.

The best shopping is down the road in Bishop. The road in and out is good and fast. Bishop (named for Samuel A. Bishop, one of the area's original cattle ranchers) is a cow town recently encased in an ugly, fat pocket of fast-food franchises. Fortunately, Schat's Dutch Bakery is there for sheepherder bread; Jack's Waffle Shop is open for breakfast with locals and cowpokes; the Firehouse Grill still attracts tourists; and the Meadow Farms Country Smokehouse (north on U.S. 395) still sells mahogany smoked slab jerky, sweet 'n' hot jerky, cheddar jerky, and other varieties, so you can gnaw your merry way through the High Sierras!

KEY INFORMATION

Four Jeffrey Campground or Sabrina Campground
Inyo National Forest
873 North Main Street
Bishop, CA 93514

Operated by: U.S. Forest Service

Information: (760) 873-2500; www.r5.fs.fed.us/inyo

Open: April to October

Individual sites: 106

Each site has: Picnic tables, fireplace

Registration: At entrance

Facilities: Water, flush toilets

Parking: At site

Fee: $12

Elevation: 8,100 feet

Restrictions:

Pets—On leash only

Fires—In fireplace

Vehicles—RVs up to 22 feet

To get there: from L.A., take I-5 north to CA 14. Go north to U.S. 395 near Inyokern. Continue north on U.S. 395 for 123 miles to Bishop. From Bishop, drive 13 miles south on CA 168 to South Lake Road. Go left and drive a mile or so to Four Jeffrey Campground. Sabrina Campground is another 4 miles south on CA 168 from that turnoff.

HORSE MEADOW CAMPGROUND

Salmon Creek, Sequoia National Forest

Horse Meadow Campground is my favorite campground. I don't even know why. Maybe it's the long grind up the mountains or the terrain, that dry, big-sky-country look with the pines, boulders, and open, green meadows. Maybe I watched too many westerns when I was a child. The sky at Horse Meadow Campground just seems a little bit bluer.

The campsites at Horse Meadow are roomy and offer a great view. Salmon Creek runs through the campground and gurgles just enough to lull you to sleep. Below the meadow, it gathers in pools deep enough for you to take a freezing dip. When you hop out, warm yourself on the hot granite slabs.

Getting to Horse Meadow is part of the fun. Pass McNally's Hamburger Stand near Fairview Campground on your way north of Kernville. You're into the wilderness now, so stock up while you can. Here, the canyon narrows, and you see cliffs of metamorphic rock colored by chartreuse lichen. Notice the tailings from Fairview Mine across the river. This is gold country. Pass Roads End (this was the road's end until 1939) and soon enough you turn right on Sherman Pass Road.

Sherman Pass Road heads up past buck brush, mountain mahogany, and fremontia, into chaparral with gray and pinyon pine, and finally, into Jeffrey pine, black oak, cedar, and white fir as you turn right on

CAMPGROUND RATINGS

Beauty: ★★★★★
Site privacy: ★★
Site spaciousness: ★★★
Quiet: ★★★★
Security: ★★★
Cleanliness/upkeep: ★★★★

This is my favorite tent campground. It's difficult to get up here, but it's worth it for the beauty and solitude.

Cherry Hill Road. It's about 10 miles up to Horse Meadow Campground, past Alder and Brush Creeks, then Poison Meadow (note the dispersed camping sites, which require a fire permit). At the junction with Horse Meadow Road, go right 1.3 miles and you're in a tent-camping paradise.

The campground has two loops. The right loop is for tent camping only and runs along a hill above Salmon Creek and the meadow. The left loop is for tenters and small RVs. The last time I was there in July, most of the folks were tent campers. The narrow ascents up Sherman Pass and Cherry Hill Roads deter RVs and trailers. And, once you're up here, it's a long, long way down for supplies. There is good water (phone the Ranger Station before coming to make sure), but no trash bins. Haul out your garbage.

Horse Meadow is a good place to bring children. The campground loops are fine for biking, and Salmon Creek offers good trout fishing, but it's not wild and dangerous like the Kern. There are many easy hikes around the meadow, including several along Salmon Creek to some good dipping pools.

To find the upper bathing pools, go to the south side of the Horse Meadow Campground's main loop and find the trail that parallels the creek. Walk east along the left bank of the creek. Cross a spur road over Salmon Creek and keep climbing; follow the creek, and you'll come to the pools.

To visit the downstream pools, walk back past the camp entrance and go left down Salmon Falls Trail. Follow the signed trail from the parking lot and skirt the meadow. When the trail crosses Salmon Creek on a big log and goes left around a rocky butte, don't follow it. Instead, head west down the right side of the creek. The trail meanders along over rocky areas, bypassing clumps of willows, and leads you past some prime pools for dipping. The water is frigid, but the sun is blazing hot. This is heaven!

For a major hike, go back to the big log crossing Salmon Creek. With a backpack filled with soda and sandwiches, head around the rocky butte toward the Salmon Creek Falls. The trail skirts the meadow and then heads into the woods. It crosses canyons while following the south side of Salmon Creek through purple lupine country with monks hood, larkspur, and red bugler. Down by the creek, you'll see willows and dogwood.

The trail continues down to the north side of Salmon Creek and ends with a view of the Greenhorn Mountains. Those more agile than I can rock hop down to the creek where there are more wonderful pools for bathing. Just beyond them, you'll find the top of Salmon Creek Falls. Rumor has it there used to be a trail down to the Kern and the base of Salmon Creek Falls.

KEY INFORMATION

Horse Meadow Campgroun, Sequoia National Forest Cannell Meadow Ranger District

105 Whitney Road, P.O. Box 9 Kernville, CA 93238

Operated by: U.S.Forest Service

Information: (760) 376-3781; www.r5.fs.fed.us/sequoia

Open: June to November

Individual sites: 18 sites for tents only, 15 sites for tents or RVs up to 23 feet long

Each site has: Picnic table, fireplace, Water (phone ahead to make sure)

Registration: At entrance

Facilities: Vault toilets

Parking: At site

Fee: $5

Elevation: 7,600 feet

Restrictions:

Pets—On leash only

Fires—In fireplaces

Vehicles—Trailers not recommended

To get there: from L.A., take I-5 north over the Tejon Pass to CA 99. Drive north on CA 99 past Bakersfield. Take CA 178 east to Lake Isabella. Take CA 155 to Wofford Heights. Bear right to Kernville. From Kernville, drive north on Sierra Way 19.4 miles and turn right on Sherman Pass Road, signed "Highway 395-Black Rock Ranger Station." Drive 6 miles and turn right on Cherry Hill Road, signed "Horse Meadow–Big Meadow." Drive up 9.1 miles on the surfaced (sometimes dirt) road to the signed campground entrance road on the right. The campground itself is 1.3 miles down the hill.

LOWER PEPPERMINT CAMPGROUND / CAMP 6 FIRE SAFE AREA

Peppermint Creek , Sequoia National Forest

L ower Peppermint and Camp 6 are a few hundred yards apart and smack dab in the middle of great Northern Sierra camping near the spectacular scenery of Dome Rock and The Needles. On your way, obtain a fire permit because it increases your camping possibilities a hundredfold. You can get one from Greenhorn Ranger Station on CA 155, at Lake Isabella, a few miles east of Bakersfield, or at Cannell Meadow Ranger Station in Kernville. The free permit allows you to camp almost anywhere in Sequoia National Forest.

Sequoia National Forest calls this dispersed camping, meaning you can camp anywhere not posted off limits. For example around Lloyd Meadow Road dozens of old logging roads or turnoffs allow you to drive a few hundred yards and camp in a private area. Of course, you'll be expected to follow the forest's regulations—cart out your garbage, dig cat holes for bodily waste, and burn your toilet paper. Try not to leave any traces of your visit.

Buy groceries in Lake Isabella or Kernville. Once you get on Lloyd Meadows Road, there are no supplies available except beer, soda, and small bags of ice at the Johnsondale R-Ranch (turn off Parker Pass Drive 0.6 mile east of the Lloyd Meadows Road). You'll pass a cowboy guard at the gate; tell him you want to shop at the store, and he'll wave you on. The R-Ranch is a private campground. The lifetime

CAMPGROUND RATINGS

Beauty: ★★★★
Site privacy: ★★★★
Site spaciousness: ★★★★
Quiet: ★★★★★
Security: ★★★★
Cleanliness/upkeep: ★★★★★

The Lower Peppermint/Camp 6 area is astonishingly beautiful, with waterslides, waterfalls, and mountain peaks. Bring bikes for good cycling along the untrafficked Lloyd Meadows Road.

membership fee is $12,500,
which gives access to cabins,
horses, RVs, trails, etc.

Winding Lloyd Meadows
Road passes through pine,
white fir, cedar, and oak
where there is water and
manzanita, fremontia, and
digger pine where it's dry.
Note turnoffs to the num-
bered Fire Safe Area Camps,
which offer good camping
(a fire permit is required to
camp in Fire Safe Areas as in
all dispersed areas). During
dry spells dispersed camping is confined to these areas
only.

Lower Peppermint Campground is a small, pretty campground mostly fre-
quented by tent campers. When I last visited, in July, there was no potable
water, so carry plenty of drinking water or plan on purifying the water from
Peppermint Creek. Boy Scouts from nearby Camp Whitsett maintain Lower
Peppermint in return for the user fees on their own camp. The sites that back up
to the creek are lovely. If these are taken, drive a few hundred yards north, then
head down the dirt road signed for Camp 6. Here, you can camp down by the
Peppermint Creek or on the bluff overlooking piney meadows, a spectacular
waterfall, and the Kern River below.

For a great hike and swim, scramble down the bluff to the foot of the falls.
Stop and swim there, or bear left along the creek until you strike a trail that
takes you east. It forks south to another area of rocky pools and cascades perfect for picnicking, swimming, and sunbathing.

However, the water runs stronger than it seems, and the wet rocks by the
stream are slick. The dry granite slabs above are just as bad. The granite
decomposes, and the little dry bits are like ball bearings.

Another good water hike leads to the Alder Slabs. Wear clothes you don't care about, because this trip involves sliding down water chutes into cold pools on your behind. It's fun! Backtrack south on Lloyd Meadows Road and park by gated Sequoia National Forest Road 22S83. Walk north on the dirt road and then turn right down a path to Alder Creek.

Alternately, drive north from Lower Peppermint Campground to see The Needles. These amazing rock formations are crystals formed under pressure from molten rock. Pushed up, The Needles cooled along vertical master joints. Ice and erosion have done the rest. Farther north, see the Freeman Creek Grove of sequoias. En route, investigate the little intersecting roads for good future camping sites. In the dead of summer, you might want to be near water, but in the late spring, this area is so beautiful it doesn't matter where you camp. You'll be blown away by the sight of all the flowers.

Bring a saw for wood gathering, and don't forget a trowel for cat holes. I often bring a leaf rake with a sawed-off handle for clearing debris around the picnic tables and fire rings and a shovel for fire control and digging out if the car gets stuck. Remember to phone ahead to check about potable water.

To get there: from L.A., take I-5 north over the Tejon Pass to CA 99. Drive north on CA 99 past Bakersfield. Take CA 178 east to Lake Isabella. Take CA 155 to Wofford Heights. Bear right to Kernville. From Kernville, drive north on Sierra Way 19.4 miles and turn left on Parker Pass Drive. It is 4.9 miles to the right-hand turn onto Lloyd Meadows Road (Forest Service Road 22S82). Drive north 13.4 miles to Lower Peppermint Campground. Camp 6 is a few hundred yards north on the right.

KEY INFORMATION

Lower Peppermint Campground or Camp 6 Fire Safe Area, Sequoia National Forest

Hot Springs Ranger District 32588 Highway 190 Springville, CA 93265

Operated by: U.S.Forest Service

Information: (559)539-2607 or (559) 784-1500; www.r5.fs.fed.us/sequoia

Open: May to October

Individual sites: 17

Each site has: Picnic table, fireplace, Water (phone ahead)

Registration: At entrance

Facilities: Vault toilets

Parking: At site

Fee: $12

Elevation: 5,300 feet

Restrictions:

Pets—Allowed

Fires—In fireplaces

Vehicles—Trailers not recommended

Other—Fire permit required for Camp 6 Fire Safe Area

MINARET FALLS CAMPGROUND

Upper San Joaquin River, Inyo National Forest

Minaret Falls Campground is the prettiest in a string of beautiful, popular campgrounds on the Upper San Joaquin River west of Mammoth Mountain. When you drive down the dirt road into the campground, silvery Minaret Falls leaps out at you. Even in late September, on my last visit, the water cascaded down the mountainside like streams of crystal.

Right away, my wife and I drove into a campsite with a clean and soft tent pitch shrouded by trees. Through the willows we could see the riverbank and the falls.

We drove a few miles up the road to Red's Meadow store and cafe to buy worms and salmon eggs for trout fishing. A little bear was raiding the back room of the store, but the clerk and a tourist scared him away. A dog lunged at the end of his leash, barking at the little bear as he scurried off.

We learned that the original Red was a gold miner who turned to tourism when the Depression and falling gold prices drove him out of business. His pack station at Red's Meadow was one of the first tourist draws in the Mammoth area.

We hiked the 1.25 miles down to Rainbow Falls along with a passel of other folks. We took the rough stairs down to the exquisite falls and stood in the spray. A rainbow arced through the mist.

We hiked back through an area of firs, lodgepoles, and Jeffrey pines, scarred like most of Devil's Postpile National Mon-

CAMPGROUND RATINGS

Beauty: ★★★★★
Site privacy: ★★★
Site spaciousness: ★★★★★
Quiet: ★★★★★
Security: ★★★★★
Cleanliness/upkeep: ★★★★

Minaret Falls Campground is the most beautiful campground in a string of popular campgrounds along the Upper San Joaquin River. Come in the fall for good fishing.

ument by a 1992 wildfire. Following the fire, rangers walked through the burn to assess the damage, and charred trees crashed down around them. It wasn't safe to walk there for months.

Back at the Minaret Campground we floated salmon eggs and earthworms down the river and caught six trout. My wife wrapped them in aluminum foil with herbs and cooked them over the campfire. It was a beautiful night. The Southern Sierras have hundreds of shooting stars.

Sleeping that night in our tent, I heard the rustle of a visitor—a bear. He ran away when I got up. I inspected the damage. My two treasured inflatable Basic Designs sinks, which my wife and I use to wash the dishes, were ruined. The bear had bitten a big hole in each of them. To add insult to injury, he also bit into my plastic collapsible water jug. Were these acts of rancor, or did he think they were full of food?

A neighbor came over. The bear had tried to open the hatch of his Nissan Z; the telltale paw marks gave the intruder away. I told him about my sinks. He recommended wiping sinks, picnic tables, and cooler tops each night with Clorox. Bears like soap; bears like everything except Clorox. I went back to my sleeping bag and heard the bear slouch through the camp again.

The next morning we walked north along the river and crossed on a log at the end of the campground. There's a short trail to the foot of Minaret Falls. We bushwhacked up to the top of the falls and dipped in some nice pools.

Later, we hiked up to Shadow Lake. It's no easy climb (round-trip is about 7 miles), but you'll agree it's worth it when you see beautiful blue Shadow Lake against huge, craggy Mount Ritter. To find the trailhead, drive back toward Mammoth from the Minaret Falls Campground. Take the road to Agnew Meadows Campground. About .3 mile in, you'll find trailhead parking with toilets and drinking water. Follow the signs to Shadow Lake, through another parking lot and across a creek to another trail juction at about 1 mile. To the left is Red's Meadow. To the right is Shadow Lake. With Mammoth Mountain at your back, climb up past Olaine Lake, cross the San Joaquin River on a wooden bridge, and hump it up the canyon wall to Shadow Lake. You'll find good fishing, so bring your fishing gear and bait.

Minaret Falls Campground is popular. Be sure to phone rangers ahead of time to make sure it's open and see how crowded it will be. Try to plan a trip before or after the prime summertime season and arrive on Thursday if you want to spend the weekend. The area is so popular that during the summertime hikers (not campers) are required to park their cars at the Mammoth Ski Resort and take an intravalley shuttle down.

You have 30 minutes from the time you occupy a campsite to pay. Park your car at the first empty campsite you find and use that 30 minutes to walk around and see if you like another site better. If you find one, leave something on the picnic table and go move your car.

To get there: from L.A., take I-5 north to CA 14. Take CA 14 north to U.S. 395 near Inyokern. Continue north on U.S. 395 for 123 miles to Bishop. Continue another 37 miles on U.S. 395 to Mammoth Lakes. From Mammoth Lakes, drive 16 miles west on Highway 203 (Minaret Summit Road) to the campground.

KEY INFORMATION

Minaret Falls Campground
Inyo National Forest
873 North Main Street
Bishop, CA 93514

Operated by: U.S. Forest Service

Information: (760) 924-5500; www.r5.fs.fed.us/inyo

Open: June to September

Individual sites: 27

Each site has: Picnic table, fireplace

Registration: At entrance

Facilities: Water, chemical toilets

Parking: At site

Fee: $14

Elevation: 7,600 feet

Restrictions:

Pets—On leash only

Fires—In fireplace

Vehicles—RVs up to 22 feet

Other—No dispersed camping in this area

MORAINE CAMPGROUND

Cedar Grove, Kings Canyon National Park

Everybody but Andrew Marvell, the 17th-century English poet, loves mountains. He called them "ill-designed excrescences" (abnormal growths). Of course, Andrew was a flatlander who never visited Kings Canyon National Park.

William Brewer did, however, and waxed eloquently about the Moraine Campground area in 1864: "...this is the grandest canyon I have ever seen. A pretty valley or flat half a mile wide lies along the river covered with trees. On both sides rise tremendous granite precipices, of every shape, often nearly perpendicular, rising from 2,500 feet to above 4,000 feet. They did not form a continuous wall, but rose in high points, with canyons coming down here and there, and with fissures, gashes, and gorges. The whole scene was sublime."

It is sublime. And it's the mountains, not the standard National Park–issue campground, that elicit this feeling. You would not come to Moraine Campground if it were not below Sentinel Ridge and Monarch Divide. However, just the spectacular drive justifies a visit. Take the wide and well banked convict-built CA 180 all the way in from Fresno. Coming over the rise to see the gorge and the mountains behind it takes your breath away. Then, circle down and follow the river to Cedar Grove and Moraine Campground.

There is a store at Cedar Grove that sells ice, beverages, and some food, and there is

CAMPGROUND RATINGS

Beauty:	★★★★★
Site privacy:	★★★
Site spaciousness:	★★★★
Quiet:	★★★★★
Security:	★★★★
Cleanliness/upkeep:	★★★★★

Moraine Campground combines a grand canyon and a pretty valley for sublime scenery. Don't miss the sensational hiking.

a cafeteria for folks tired of camp cooking. There are hot showers and a laundromat. For an ice cream or a sandwich, stop at Kings Canyon Lodge on the way in or out, approximately halfway between Grants Grove and Cedar Grove. The charming lodge is rustic, but beautiful, with flower beds mixed in with old, rusted mining equipment. The little cabins were authentic dwellings of early 20th-century miners.

A little farther on is Boyden Cavern. I plunked down my $6 for the guided tour. Native Americans avoided the place, feeling that bad spirits lived there. I can see why. I swallowed hard when the guide turned off the lights and described the mile or so of solid granite over our heads. The children on the tour were thrilled.

Another fun activity for children at Cedar Grove is a horse ride at Cedar Grove Pack Station. Here, you can arrange anything from a one-hour ride to a week-long trip into the backcountry. They offer kiddy rides as well. If you come to camp and want to arrange a more elaborate ride, it's best to phone ahead and make reservations. Call (559) 565-3464.

The river was running too fast for much fishing the last time I was at Cedar Grove in August. However, the cowboys at the stables told me you could do all right if you knew where to fish. "Where's that?" I asked, but they laughed and wouldn't disclose any information.

Upriver from Moraine, there are several parking areas where you can pull over and walk down to the river. The second or third areas access a part of the river where the current runs languidly even at flood tide. I wonder if this is the cowboy fishing hole? I got my lure wet, but there were no trout takers.

Farther on, past the bridge on the left, you'll find the beginning of the Cedar Grove Motor Nature Trail, a dirt road that heads back to Cedar Grove Village across the North Fork Kings River. It passes several great places to park and hang out down by the water.

You can't leave Cedar Grove without hiking up to Mist Falls. The trailhead is at Roads End, about 6 miles from the Ranger Station in Cedar Grove. Right away, you'll cross Copper Creek, near the site of a former Native American village. Look carefully and you'll find flakes of obsidian, which Native Americans used to make weapons and tools. There was a store here once, and John Muir swore by the pies the owner's wife, Viola, made. About 2 miles in, head uphill following the river. On your left is Buck Peak (8,776 feet), and The Sphinx (9,146 feet) is behind you. See if you can sort out the ponderosa, Jeffrey, and sugar pines. To the east, don't miss the waterfall on Gardiner Creek. Soon enough, you'll reach Mist Falls, and the sight is worth the climb.

The best time to visit Moraine Campground at Cedar Grove is in the spring. It's cool enough then to hike comfortably all day long, and and the crowds haven't begun to arrive in droves, as in August. Still, Kings Canyon National Park is beautiful any month of the year.

KEY INFORMATION

Moraine Campground
Kings Canyon National Park
47050 Generals Highway
Three Rivers, CA 93271-9651
Operated by: National Park Service

Information: (559) 565-3341; www.nps.gov/seki

Open: June to October (depending on road and snow conditions)

Individual sites: 120

Each site has: Picnic table, fire pit, bear box

Registration: At entrance

Facilities: Water, flush toilets

Parking: At site

Fee: $14

Elevation: 4,600 feet

Restrictions:

Pets—On leash only

Fires—In fire pits

Vehicles—Two per site maximum

Other—Six campers per site maximum

To get there: from L.A., take I-5 north over the Tejon Pass to CA 99. Drive north on CA 99 past Bakersfield 104 miles to Fresno. Go east on CA 180 to Kings Canyon National Park. Follow CA 180 for 29 miles to Cedar Grove Village. From Cedar Grove Village in Kings Canyon Park drive east on CA 180 for 1 mile to the campground.

PRINCESS CAMPGROUND

Hume, Sequoia National Forest

You'll love Princess Campground just like you love a golden retriever for being a basic, good dog. Princess is a campground's campground. Set under the shade of second-growth sequoias and pines, Princess is covered on one flank by a shimmering alpine meadow. The campsites are private and level, and everything is well maintained and clean.

Hume Lake, 3 miles down the road, is a big draw for anybody with a vinyl water toy or a fishing rod. A huge Christian campground occupies one end of the lake's shoreline. Dammed up by lumber folks, Hume Lake supplied the water for the flume that scooted timber down to Sanger in the San Joaquin Valley 54 miles away. Flumes work on the same principle as water slides: water reduces friction.

Unlike the water in the mountain streams, Hume Lake warms up enough that you can actually swim without turning gelid. A path encircles the lake, and you can find your own grassy beach spot. Air mattresses or inexpensive blow-up boats are big hits. I saw people catching edible-sized fish as well.

A choice spot is Sandy Cove Beach. Coming down from CA 180, pass Hume Lake Campground and follow the road around past the Powder Canyon Picnic Area, through the Hume Lake Christian Camp, and along Lakeshore Drive to Sandy Cove Beach. This is a fun and safe place to swim,

CAMPGROUND RATINGS

Beauty: ★★★★
Site privacy: ★★★★
Site spaciousness: ★★★★
Quiet: ★★★
Security: ★★★
Cleanliness/upkeep: ★★★★

Princess Campground has everything—big trees, warm lakes, and fantastic gorge views. Come for a week with the family.

where the trill of youthful swimmers' voices resounds. Adults with more secluded sun bathing in mind can follow Landslide Creek up to find a private spot. The road that heads south to Generals Highway follows the creek most of the way.

Princess is regarded as an overflow campground for Hume Lake, but I find it offers much better camping. It's quieter and cleaner, and because you have to walk downhill to the lake from Hume Lake Campground, you might as well drive down from Princess. At least up there you won't suffer the incessant camp counselors' whistles in the morning. And the added 700 feet of elevation at Princess cuts down on the bugs and the dust.

The Indian Basin Grove Trail is an easy one-hour hike, starting about half a mile west of the Princess Campground entrance. You can walk there from Princess or take a car and park in a turnout just west of the road. The trail follows Forest Service Road 13S50 north through ponderosas and cedars. Look for the sequoia stumps, then for the second-generation sequoias growing back. After a mile or so, pass Forest Service Road 13S07, which could take you back to Princess Campground, but persevere and follow the road north to a ridge. When the road turns east, find the trail in a patch of manzanita. The trail continues north to a point overlooking Kings Canyon.

Another good hike is to the Boole Tree. Drive west on CA 180 to Forest Service Road 13S55, then drive 2.7 miles to the trailhead parking lot. Follow the signed trail. It's an easy 2-mile trip in and out. Be sure to see the tree—it's an incredible sight. Why didn't loggers ever cut it down? Nobody knows, but some say Frank Boole, general manager of the Sanger Lumber Company, spared the tree as a tribute to himself.

Just up the road is Grant Grove, with more incredible sequoias. One tree actually antedates Christ by 1,500 years. Sequoias do not die of old age; they are the closest we'll get to eternity until we go to our own rewards. The short walk out to Panoramic Point is fun, especially at sunset.

At Grant Grove Village you can buy ice, soda, and beer. Many families stay at Princess Campground. The last time I was there, I camped next to a schoolteacher and his herd of children. He was an erudite chap and taught his wee ones some games originating with the Monachi and Yokut Native Americans. Their favorite involved guessing who on the opposing team held a rock beneath an all-concealing blanket.

There are no bear boxes at Princess Campground, but there are black bears. You must be careful with your food. As soon as you eat, take the trash to the bins. Conceal your cooler in your car. The bears recognize coolers and know their purpose. Don't leave anything in your tent that has a strong odor, such as sunscreen, lipstick, skin cream, etc. Rangers shoot bears when they become repeat food raiders, so be cool and save a bear.

To get there: from L.A., take I-5 north over the Tejon Pass to CA 99. Drive north on CA 99 past Bakersfield 104 miles to Fresno. Go east on CA 180 to Kings Canyon National Park. Follow CA 180 to Grant Grove. From Grant Grove in Kings Canyon National Park, drive 6 miles north to Princess Campground on the right.

KEY INFORMATION

Princess Campground, Sequoia National Forest
Hume Lake Ranger District
35860 East Kings Canyon Road
Dunlap, CA 93621

Operated by: California Land Management

Information: (559) 338-2251; www.r5.fs.fed.us/sequoia

Open: May to September

Individual sites: 50 tent sites, 40 RV sites

Each site has: Picnic table, fireplace

Registration: At entrance; reserve by phone, (877) 444-6777, or online, www.reserveUSA.com

Facilities: Water, vault toilets

Parking: At site

Fee: $12; $8.65 nonrefundable reservation fee

Elevation: 5,900 feet

Restrictions:
Pets—On leash only
Fires—In fireplace
Vehicles—RVs up to 32 feet

THE NORTHERN SIERRAS

QUAKING ASPEN CAMPGROUND / PEPPERMINT CAMPGROUND

Ponderosa, Sequoia National Forest

Quaking Aspen Campground and its nearby neighbor, Peppermint Campground, span the entire range of camping available in this part of the Sierras. Quaking Aspen is developed, clean, well maintained, and set in a stand of red fir, *not* quaking aspen as its name infers. Peppermint Campground is situated higher among pines, cedar, and black oak and is undeveloped (a fire permit is required). Quaking Aspen lies by meadows of willow, aspen, and yarrow. Peppermint is located by Peppermint Creek, offering trout fishing and bathing in chilly pools down from the campground.

Ponderosa Lodge, between the two campgrounds, is a fun place to grab a beer and chili or to pick up ice, but don't plan on shopping there. Springville is the last port of call for supplies. This pretty little town in Tule River country has just about everything you'll need. Before Jedediah Smith trapped beaver here in 1827, the Yaudanchis (a subtribe of the Yokut) lived in the foothills during the winter and trekked to the mountains to gather food in the summer. By 1857 the Yaudanchis were history.

Settlers poured into the area. John Nelson forged his way up the canyon of the Middle Fork of the Tule River (CA 190 east of Springville today) and filed a claim on property that is now Camp Nelson. Springville (named for the soda springs in the area) was the site of a mill that

CAMPGROUND RATINGS

Beauty: ★★★★★
Site privacy: ★★★★
Site spaciousness: ★★★★
Quiet: ★★★★
Security: ★★★★★
Cleanliness/upkeep: ★★★★★

Come to Quaking Aspen Campground or its neighbor, rustic Peppermint Campground, in the fall for autumn leaves and in the summer for hiking and mountain biking.

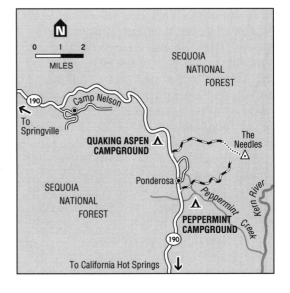

processed the raw timber that was hauled down by horse- and mule-team wagons from the higher reaches of what is today Sequoia National Forest. Logging continued into the early 1900s, when the Porterville Northeastern Railroad built a spur into Springville. Then, finished lumber, citrus fruits, and apples could be shipped to the valley below.

Now, citrus orchards dot the lower foothills leading into town along CA 190. Ranching operations spread across wide-open parcels of oak- and buckeye-studded hills. Apples are grown farther up on the cooler, protected slopes, merging into the manzanita, black oak, cedar, and pine. Logging continues under the supervision of the Sequoia National Forest.

Between Quaking Aspen Campground and Ponderosa Lodge, note the actual quaking aspens that give the campground its name. These slender trees have light bark and roundish leaves. Vivid green in spring and bright gold in fall, the leaves quiver at the least breath of breeze.

The good bathing holes on Peppermint Creek are downstream from the campground about a quarter of a mile. Stick to the south side of the creek, because it's hard to cross over from the other side. The wet rocks are extremely slippery. Don't even think of crossing on them. Find a place with a sandy bottom before you try getting in the water. Also, watch out for the granite slabs on the banks. Their surface decomposes, leaving slippery bits of rock.

A great hike is out to the Needles Lookout. It's only a 4-mile round-trip of pretty easy walking, but plan on making a day of it. Take lunch. The dirt road to the trailhead takes off to the east about one-half mile south of Ponderosa Lodge. Drive 2.8 miles in and park. The trail begins at the east end of the parking lot. Note the small purple flowers along the trail. They are called pennyroyals (*Mentha pulegium*) and are used to make mint tea. Pennyroyals are not local, however; they are a native of Europe brought in by the forty-niners.

Along the trail, look north to Kaweah peaks and Mount Whitney and northeast to the Kern Plateau peaks of Kern and Olancha. Then, keep an eye out for the lookout on top of the westernmost Needle—it's a fire tower manned in fire season.

Believe me, the view is worth the slog up the switchback ladders to the catwalk. Talk to the fire watcher if he is on duty. This place can get hairy. In storms, the lookout is frequently struck by lightning. In fact, the fire watcher has a special stool fitted with glass insulators that he sits on when there is lightning striking nearby!

The camping at Quaking Aspen Campground is especially beautiful in the fall with the turning of the leaves. I enjoyed Quaking Aspen in the summer as well. It's a very gracious place and is the birthplace of my famous one-pot Hungarian potato/hot dog stew. Saute diced onions in a little oil in a pot. Add quartered potatoes and hot paprika. Stir and cover. Simmer until potatoes are almost done, then add hot dogs and simmer. Eat. Food good.

To get there: from L.A., take I-5 north over the Tejon Pass to CA 99. Drive north on CA 99 past Bakersfield. Take CA 65 north to Porterville. Go east 17 miles on CA 190 to Springville. From Springville, drive 23.3 miles east on CA 190 to Quaking Aspen Camp-ground on the right. Peppermint Campground is 3 miles farther on the left.

KEY INFORMATION

Quaking Aspen Campground or Peppermint Campground, Sequoia National Forest

Tule River Ranger District
32588 CA 190
Springville, CA 93265
Operated by: U.S. Forest Service

Information: (559) 784-1500; (559) 539-2607; www.r5.fs.fed.us/sequoia

Open: May to November

Individual sites: 32

Each site has: Picnic table, fireplace

Registration: At entrance; reserve by phone, (877) 444-6777, or online, www.reserveUSA.com

Facilities: Water, vault toilets

Parking: At site

Fee: $14; $8.65 nonrefundable reservation fee

Elevation: 7,000 feet

Restrictions:

Pets—On leash only

Fires—In fireplaces

Vehicles—RVs up to 27 feet

Other—Fire permit required for Peppermint Campground; 2 wheelchair-accessible sites available

RANCHERIA CAMPGROUND

Huntington Lake, Sierra National Forest

Rancheria Campground on Huntington Lake is big, handsome, and noisy. The acoustics around camp on the pine-shored lake are such that you can hear a mouse belch at dusk from the south shore. You'll hear folks laughing on boats at the nearby marina, outboards putting on fishing skiffs, chaps hammering siding on cottages by the town of Lake Shore, and the occasional Fire Service helicopter fly-by. It feels like one big, beautiful neighborhood.

The campground has been around for a long time, and the sites are screened by pine and brush. Many are walk-ins along the lake, allowing you to pitch your tent right on the shore. Folks with boats can tie them to a root next to their campsite. The beach slopes gently into the water, which makes for good wading. There are sites back in the woods, too, for people who want to avoid all the aquatic activity.

Perched on the edge of the wilderness, Huntington Lake is a good first camp for anyone heading farther in to Thomas A. Edison Lake (a.k.a. Edison Lake) or Florence Lake. You'll find last-chance shopping at the country store in Lake Shore and information at the Ranger Station. There's a good chance that you will want to settle in at Rancheria and forget the hairy drive up over Kaiser Pass.

The lakes in this region comprise the Big Creek hydroelectric project, owned by Southern California Edison. Water runs

CAMPGROUND RATINGS

Beauty: ★★★★
Site privacy: ★★★★
Site spaciousness: ★★★★
Quiet: ★★★★★
Security: ★★★★
Cleanliness/upkeep: ★★★★★

Though sometimes crowded, lakeside Rancheria Campground offers good, solid, safe tent camping.

from Edison and Florence lakes flows into Huntington Lake and on to Shaver Lake, turning turbines along the way.

C.B. Shaver was the first to use the power of water here when he built a millpond to saw lumber before floating it down a 40-mile flume to Clovis. When the lumber gave out, the power company moved in and built dams and reservoirs.

For a power company, water in a reservoir is like money in the bank. It provides cheap, clean, reliable power that can be used almost immediately. As long as the lakes are full, the vacationing public is happy. But, nothing is uglier than an empty lake.

You can rent boats at the marina across from Rancheria Campground. Or, visit in the winter and ski at nearby Sierra Summit Ski Resort on Chinese Peak. I found the skiing spectacular, but heard some experts complaining that the best runs were too short. Hike up to Rancheria Falls from the trailhead across the road from Rancheria Campground. Or, hike to the river pools. The trailhead is in the second parking lot of the ski resort.

There is decent shopping at Ken's Market in Shaver Lake, and you'll find beer, ice, and sundries at the friendly country store in Lake Shore. But, if you want a sirloin steak, you better bring it with you. While you're packing, it's not a bad idea to bring a pair of shoes to wear in and around the lake.

And, don't accommodate the bears! Put all edibles in your car and out of view. Bring a small bottle of Clorox and wipe down your cooking gear and picnic table before turning in. Bears don't like the smell; maybe they associate it with the toilet facilities.

When I was there in September, the bears were especially active at Lower Billy Campground on the other side of Lake Shore. I spoke to a woman at the Ranger Station, who said that a bear broke into her storage shed a few nights before and ate everything but some frozen ears of corn. That was at 3:14 A.M. The next night, the bear came back at exactly 3:14 A.M. for the frozen corn.

Be sure to read the memorial on the rock by the Ranger Station. It honors a crew of airmen who died in 1944. Apparently, a B-24 bomber ran into trouble. The pilot gave the crew two options—bail out or stay with the ship and gut it out. Two men jumped and lived. The plane disappeared into the blue and was lost for a decade. Finally, in 1955, the power company lowered the water in Huntington Lake to make some repairs on the dam. The receding water revealed the wreckage of the missing B-24 and the bodies of the remaining crew members.

I thought of those young men as I swam in azure Huntington Lake and stood in the mist from the generator turbines by the Kaiser Pass Road. Maybe it would be better if they hadn't been found. Then, we could always think of them out there somewhere, handsome and young in sheepskin flying jackets, their faces full of promise.

To get there: from L.A., take I-5 north over the Tejon Pass to CA 99. Drive north on CA 99 past Bakersfield 104 miles to Fresno. Take CA 41 north to CA 168. Go northeast to Shaver Lake. From Shaver Lake, head 20 miles north on CA 168. Rancheria Campground is on the left as you come to the head of Huntington Lake.

KEY INFORMATION

Rancheria Campground, Sierra National Forest
Supervisor's Office
P.O. Box 559
Prather, CA 93651
(559) 297-0706
Operated by: California Land Management

Information: (559) 855-5355; www.r5.fs.fed.us/sierra; California Road Conditions (CALTRANS), (800) 427-7673

Open: All year

Individual sites: 149 sites (some tents only)

Each site has: Picnic table, fire ring, parking spur

Registration: At entrance; reserve by phone, (877) 444-6777, or online, www.reserveUSA.com

Facilities: Water, flush and vault toilets

Parking: At or near site

Fee: $14–22; $8.65 nonrefundable reservation fee

Elevation: 7,000 feet

Restrictions:

Pets—On leash only

Fires—In fireplace

Vehicles—RVs up to 40 feet

Other—Camp in color-coded sites—yellow for tents, blue for RVs up to 20 feet, white for RVs up to 30 feet, red for RVs up to 40 feet

REDWOOD MEADOW CAMPGROUND

Fairview, Sequoia National Forest

If campgrounds could have expressions, then Redwood Meadow would have a smiling face. This is an easy campground to like. The facilities are clean and well maintained. The sites are under well-spaced trees allowing shadow and sunlight with lots of room for tent pitches. Below is a big meadow with flowers that fills the world with light. All this, and the campground is not that crowded. There are so many free surrounding campgrounds, as well as a lot of dispersed camping, that Redwood Meadow doesn't get hit hard. But for me, it's worth the bucks to stay in this happy campground with the Trail of 100 Giants just across the road.

The Trail of 100 Giants is a great place to get acquainted with the "Big Trees." The largest tree in the grove has a diameter of 20 feet and is 220 feet in height. The trees' ages range between 500 to 1,500 years old. These old guys were babes when the Roman Empire fell.

Back in the glacial eras, the giant sequoias (*Sequoiadendron gigantuem*) grew all over what is now the western United States. When the climate dried out, the sequoias retreated to ecological islands with abundant rainfall and runoff, where they grow mostly in granite basins or where bedrock is near the surface.

Try to burn a piece of redwood bark and you'll see how resistant it is to fire. The bark is impregnated with tannins that are

CAMPGROUND RATINGS

Beauty: ★★★★★

Site privacy: ★★★

Site spaciousness: ★★★★

Quiet: ★★★★

Security: ★★★

Cleanliness/upkeep: ★★★★

A happy campground with the Trail of 100 Giants and a meadow full of flowers. You can't beat it.

resistant to both fire and insects. That allows the trees to grow very old. And, given abundant moisture, Redwoods are the fastest-growing trees in the United States. Age and growth rate explain why the giant sequoias are so huge.

For years, foresters tried to protect the giant sequoia from fire. Only recently did they realize that the sequoias need fire to perpetuate. Ground fires do not burn through the bark, but the rising heat opens the cones, which remain on the trees for up to 20 years. When the cones open, the seeds fall on the soft, recently burned earth. When it rains, these seeds germinate in the sunlight that shines to the ground freely through the recently burned foliage.

An interesting friend of the giant sequoia is the giant carpenter ant who makes nests in the sequoias by hollowing them out. Try not to think about the ant when you're standing under a giant sequoia and pray for an occasional fire, since it reduces the population of the giant ants.

For bicycling, Western Divide Highway is a great option. The road is wide with no blind curves. On a weekday you'll hardly see a car. A good tour is from Redwood Meadow Campground to Ponderosa Lodge and back. The round-trip is about 24 miles. You'll bike from good clear water available at the campground to the Ponderosa Lodge's varied liquid refreshments and breakfast, lunch, and dinner choices, then back home again to the campground. On the way, a short section of dirt road takes you to Dome Rock—be sure to stop. A quick walk along an obvious path will lead you to a spectacular view. Look down and you'll see the slash of Kern Canyon. Spot The Needles, Peppermint

Creek, and Lower Peppermint Campground below. What a wild, lovely vista!

Another great mountain-bike trip is down the connector road that heads left from Western Divide Highway about 3 to 4 miles from Redwood Campground. It climbs Nobe Creek basin to Windy Gap, then passes Coy Flat Campground, and ends up at Camp Nelson (about 24 miles one way). I found the trip out to be quite long, and was greatly relieved when someone in our party hitched a ride on a pickup truck back to Redwood Campground to get a relief vehicle.

Reserve a site at Redwood Meadow Campground on big weekends. I especially like sites #2 through #8 because they are off the highway and backed down to the little stream. If the campground is too busy, head north a half mile on Western Divide Highway. To the right is a dirt road leading down to Long Meadow Campground, a delightful place to pitch a tent. (Get a fire permit from the Ranger Station—it's good for the year!) Or, try Holey Meadow Campground. Or, head back to Parker Pass Road and go east. Almost immediately, you'll find turnoffs to good dispersed camping on the right by the stream. Armed with a fire permit, you can find great camping spots anytime in this area.

KEY INFORMATION

Redwood Meadow Campground, Sequoia National Forest

Hot Springs Ranger District

32588 Highway 190

Springville, CA 93265

Operated by: California Land Management

Information: (559) 539-2607 or (559) 784-1500; www.r5.fs.fed.us/sequoia

Open: June to September

Individual sites: 15

Each site has: Picnic table, fireplace, Water (phone ahead)

Registration: At entrance; reserve by phone, (877) 444-6777, or online, www.reserveUSA.com

Facilities: Vault toilets

Parking: At site

Fee: $14; $8.65 nonrefundable reservation fee

Elevation: 6,500 feet

Restrictions:

Pets—Allowed

Fires—In fireplaces

Vehicles—RVs up to 16 feet

To get there: from L.A., take I-5 north over the Tejon Pass to CA 99. Drive north on CA 99 past Bakersfield. Take CA 178 east to Lake Isabella. Take CA 155 to Wofford Heights. Bear right to Kernville. From Kernville, drive north on Sierra Way 19.4 miles and turn left on Parker Pass Road. Drive 10.4 miles to Western Divide Highway. Go right (north) and Redwood Meadow Campground is 3 miles up on the right.

SHAKE CAMP CAMPGROUND
Mountain Home State Forest

Shake Camp Campground will satisfy the buckaroo in you and your children. This place is about horses and the wild, open western sky. The campground itself is small, but well maintained. The campsites are roomy and fairly private down in a valley between Moses and Maggie mountains. There's an abundance of pine-needled pitches on which to set your tent. This is the best base camp for exploring Mountain Home State Forest.

Perched on the edge of the Golden Trout Wilderness, Mountain Home State Forest is virtually unknown. When I was last there in August, I saw very few backpackers or campers. Most visitors were fishing in the few stocked ponds, frolicking with their children in the Tule River at Hidden Falls, or getting ready to take horses back into the Sierra high country for an incredible adventure.

A few hundred yards down the road is the Balch Park Pack Station, where I spoke with a young cowpoke who painted a glowing picture of wonderful high lakes full of golden trout and alpine meadows under rugged peaks. You can rent horses, pack animals, and a cowpoke packer to take you up to these incredible backcountry campsites and loll around for as many days as you desire. On the predetermined day, the whole circus comes back for you. By this time, your saddle sores will have mended enough to enjoy the return ride as

CAMPGROUND RATINGS

Beauty: ★★★★
Site privacy: ★★★★
Site spaciousness: ★★★★★
Quiet: ★★★★★
Security: ★★★
Cleanliness/upkeep: ★★★★

Shake Camp Campground has horses, big trees, and the expansive western sky. Plan ahead—bring ice.

well. We figured about $150 per person for four people; this includes one day in, one day out, and as many days as you want camping. A pretty good deal.

Balch Park Pack Station also arranges all-inclusive trips on which they provide everything—packer, equipment, stock, cook, food, etc. Of course, the pack station also offers all-day rides from the stable with a guide and pack horse for $50 per day per person. Phone ahead for reservations at (209) 539-2227.

Between the pack station and the campground, there are public corrals for privately owned horses and parking lots for trailers. Many of the horse owners and the folks renting from Balch Park Pack Station stay at the campground, so it's a horsey lot. I met some fun-loving, yet responsible people who live for their animals.

If Shake Camp is full, and you don't want to take the backcountry horse-trekking option, try Frasier Mill Campground down the road. It offers good camping if you don't mind the darkness-at-noon aspect of the forest there. Forget Balch County Park; it's dusty as hell, and the campsites feel like parking places at a drive-in theater. Great springtime camping can be found at Hidden Falls on the Tule; however, when school is out, the place is overrun with roving packs of teenage campers wielding fishing rods.

A great hike from Shake Camp Campground is down the Moses Gulch Trail. Round-trip is around 7 miles. We took about five hours to do the loop, but this included lunch and a dip in the North Fork Middle Fork Tule River. Basically, the hike takes you down to Moses Gulch Campground, up to Hidden Falls Campground, and farther up along the river trail. Ford the river at Redwood

Crossing and head northwest, then south to Shake Camp Campground. Obtain the USGA 7.5 minute maps for Camp Wishon and Moses Mountain for this trip.

A shorter loop hike begins across from the public corrals and heads west up the hill to the giant sequoia, Adam Tree. Farther ahead is the Eve Tree, killed by loggers who stripped the bark off with axes. Why? Nobody knows. Cross a gulch and a stream, and you'll see some California hazelnuts growing near the sequoias. Look for the nuts in the fall. (Native Americans ground the nuts to make bread.) Carry on to the granite boulder signed "Indian Bathtubs" and scramble to the top to find oversized acorn mortar holes. Why are they oversized? Nobody knows. From there, the trail heads south through cedar and fir and comes out where you started.

Think about fishing for the native golden trout, the California state freshwater fish. How did the golden trout reach the southern Sierra? They probably came up the San Joaquin River when high water in the Great Central Valley would push the Kern River via Tule Lake into the San Joaquin. All other trout in high-country lakes are stock trout. The only other native, the Kern River rainbow trout, is actually a golden trout with different markings.

Remember—Mountain Home State Forest is isolated. There is no store on the mountain. The nearest stores are in Springville, so bring everything you need. Use block ice, since it lasts three times longer than cube ice. It's not a bad idea to bring an extra sealed cooler of ice to replenish your regular cooler when it runs out. Fuel up before you head into the mountains.

KEY INFORMATION

Shake Camp Campground
Mountain Home State Forest
P.O. Box 517
Springfield, CA 93265

Operated by: California Department of Forestry and Fire Prevention

Information: Summer: (559) 539-2321; winter: (559) 539-2855;

Open: June to October (phone ahead for weather and road conditions)

Individual sites: 11

Each site has: Picnic table, fireplace

Registration: Not required; reservations available for groups only

Facilities: Water, vault toilets

Parking: At site

Fee: No fee

Elevation: 6,500 feet

Restrictions:

Pets—On leash only

Fires—In fireplace

Vehicles—Small RVs

To get there: from L.A., take I-5 north over the Tejon Pass to CA 99. Drive north on CA 99 past Bakersfield. Take Highway 65 north to Porterville. From Porterville, drive east on CA 190 through Springville. Then go left on Balch Park Drive for 3 miles. Turn right on Bear Creek Road and drive about 21 miles to the campground.

TILLIE CREEK CAMPGROUND

Lake Isabella, Sequoia National Forest

Tillie Creek is a campground for all seasons. I love Tillie in the fall when the leaves change, in the winter and spring when it's warm on the plateau and there's snow up above in the mountains that ring the lake, and in the summer when it's hotter than Hades and all you can do is sit by the water with a beer and a fishing pole.

I also love camping at Tillie Creek with my young niece, because Tillie Creek is very friendly to children. There's a beautiful stream running through the camp that's never fast or deep enough to carry off a child. The lake has a gradually sloping shore. The roads through the campground are just right for young cyclists. There are flushing toilets and hot showers.

This is not the forest primeval. Tillie Creek is what a scout camp or small-town park used to be 30 years ago. There are child-friendly activities in the area, and Wofford Heights is just around the corner for a quick ice cream or fast-food run.

Look out over Isabella Lake and see the watery grave of ancient Native American villages, historic towns, ranches, and farms —all now submerged. When the dam was built in 1953, water filled the Kern River Valley. When the lake is low, look for a series of snags to find the former courses of the north and south forks of the Kern.

As you drive toward present-day Kernville, note the old cemetery to the right. Around the cemetery sit the foundations

CAMPGROUND RATINGS

Beauty: ★★★★★
Site privacy: ★★★
Site spaciousness: ★★★★
Quiet: ★★★★
Security: ★★★
Cleanliness/upkeep: ★★★★

Tillie Creek is child-friendly and perfect for all seasons.

of old Kernville. When Isabella Lake was created, the
government helped relocate
the town to its present site.
To get a free map of old
Kernville, Visit the Kern Valley Museum in Kernville.

In Wofford, head east on
Evans Road to visit a site of
infamy. Park near the El
Segundo Rod and Gun Club
and climb the hill just to the
south called the Hill of Three
Crosses. Look for mortars in
the rock where once Tuba-
tulabal Native Americans
ground acorns. Here in 1863,
Captain Moses McLaughlin
and his men massacred a group of Native Americans. At the time, many felt
violence was justified. This can be the basis for a good civics lesson.

To find another historic landmark, drive south on CA 155 to the Keyesville
Road. Turn right (southwest) and drive to the end of the paved road. Turn
right towards Fort Hill to find all that remains of Keyesville. In 1850, Dickie
Keyes, a Cherokee, hit gold-bearing quartz a few hundred yards northwest up
Hogeye Gulch. To the south, the Mammoth Mine was found soon afterward
and the wild town was born. One of the local hunters who supplied the
miners with fresh meat was named Grizzly Adams, because he had two pet
grizzly bears. (Remember the TV show of the same name?) Keyesville is long
gone, save one house. Built in 1880, it was the scene of a big gunfight involving the "shootin' Walkers." Today, it is occupied and cared for by some locals.

Another interesting trip is to the South Fork Wildlife Area. Go into Kernville
and head south on Sierra Way to the wildlife area around South Fork Kern
River. Take field glasses and look for the great blue herons who nest in the
crowns of trees. Open-minded herons often share trees with owls or hawks.

South of the wildlife area are cottonwood and willow stands managed by the Nature Conservancy. The endangered yellow-billed cuckoo and the southwestern willow flycatcher supposedly nest here. I searched for an hour without luck. Apparently, the cuckoos like to eat hairy caterpillars, and the flycatchers fly so fast they are hard to see.

Marinas in the area rent boats, allowing for fun excursions. Remember to bring hats, sunscreen, food, and water. Remember, too, that shallow lakes are more prone to dangerous windblown waves than deep lakes. That has to do with the relationship between waves and the lake bottom (similarly, ocean waves grow taller as they approach the shallows near land).

How can you be in this area and not go river rafting? The trick is to marry the rafting experience with the age and daring of yourself and your companions. I've been on sedate and bucolic rafting trips and others that turned my hair white. Ask around to find an established rafting company with a solid reputation.

You'll have the most fun, however, just hanging around Tillie Creek campground. The atmosphere encourages relaxation. The playground attracts and engages children. The changing sun and breeze off the lake combine for an incredible show. Tillie is a place to bring children for a weekend and actually relax.

To get there: from L.A., take I-5 north over the Tejon Pass to CA 99. Drive north on CA 99 past Bakersfield. Take CA 178 east to Lake Isabella. Take CA 155 toward Wofford Heights on the west shore of Isabella Lake. One mile before Wofford Heights on the right is the entrance to Tillie Creek Campground.

KEY INFORMATION

Tillie Creek Campground, Sequoia National Forest Greenhorn District
P.O. Box 3810
Lake Isabella, CA 92340

Operated by: California Land Management

Information: (760) 379-5646; www.r5.fs.fed.us/sequoia

Open: All year

Individual sites: 159

Each site has: Picnic table, fire ring

Registration: Host will collect on rounds; reserve by phone, (877) 444-6777, or online, www.reserveUSA.com

Facilities: Water, flush toilets, hot showers, sanitary disposal station, playground, fish-cleaning station, RV dump station

Parking: At site

Fee: $14; $8.65 nonrefundable reservation fee

Elevation: 2,500 feet

Restrictions:

Pets—On 6-foot or shorter leash only

Fires—In fire ring

Vehicles—RVs up to 45 feet

TRAPPER SPRINGS CAMPGROUND

Courtright Reservoir, Sierra National Forest

Trapper Springs Campground is clean, uncrowded, and beautiful at a subalpine 8,200 feet. It's a land of granite peaks towering thousands of feet above thick pines, of twisted tamarack and juniper growing out of rock. Courtright Reservoir is a sparkling blue gem against the gray granite, brown tree trunks, and green pine boughs.

What an incredibly beautiful place! John Muir, Scottish sheepherder turned naturalist, wrote: "The Sierra should be called not the Nevada or Snowy Range, but the range of light. And after ten years spent in the heart of it, rejoicing and wondering, bathing in the glorious floods of light, seeing the sunbursts of morning among the icy peaks, the noonday radiance on the trees and rocks and snow, the flush of the alpenglow, and a thousand dashing waterfalls with their marvelous abundance of irised spray, it still seems to me above all others the Range of Light, the most divinely beautiful of all the mountain chains I have ever seen."

Range of Light. That thought stayed with me for the two days my wife and I spent at Trapper Springs. On the first, we walked down the trail to Courtright Reservoir, hiked across the pined granite escarpments at dusk, and drank sundowners on a rock scoured clean by ice, sun, and wind.

The next day, September 15th, hunting season began. I expected campgrounds full

CAMPGROUND RATINGS

Beauty: ★★★★★
Site privacy: ★★★★★
Site spaciousness: ★★★★★
Quiet: ★★★★★
Security: ★★★★★
Cleanliness/upkeep: ★★★★★

Trapper Springs Campground is an easy-to-access, remote, beautiful campground.

of gun-toting, beer-swigging NRA-ers; fusillades of rifle fire at dawn. Au contraire; the Trapper Springs Campground attracted just a few polite, gentlemen hunters, and there were a few far-off rifle pops, but otherwise nothing disturbed the sylvan peace of the reservoir and mountainside.

I'm not sure if this state of serenity had anything to do with Marv, our camp host, and his dog, but it's a possibility. The first night, the campground hostess came by in her golf cart, and we asked her about the hunters. She said, "Well, if they get rowdy, I send my husband Marv down to talk to them, and he takes his dog." Well, we met Marv. He looked rawhide tough, like an ex–rodeo rider, and his dog made your average pit bull look like a French poodle.

The campground was built and is run by Pacific Gas and Electric. They do a fine job. All the facilities are well maintained. The sites are all secluded and clean, and the pitches are well off the service road. The pit toilets are clean. We paid for two sites—#9 and #10—sheltered under a huge granite tor.

The campground is located well off the reservoir shore, which keeps the place relatively uncrowded. In Southern California, wherever there's water, there are people. They come for fishing, boating, swimming, and the beauty and primitive peace of mind that a stream or lake provides. So, pick a campground like Trapper Springs that's a little off the water and you won't have too many neighbors.

The trail to the reservoir leaves from the bottom of the second campground loop. The shore is about a quarter of a mile downhill. Or, you can just head north up across the granite escarpments and work your way down. A fishing trail encircles the entire reservoir. There are great places to picnic, sunbathe, and fish. If you fish, be sure to obtain a license and to wear it visibly.

Considering how remote Trapper Springs Campground feels, the road in is pretty mild. Dinkey Creek Road is wide and well graded; you'll thank God for this when you meet the heavily loaded lumber trucks. You'll pass the Ranger Station and small grocery store at Dinkey and head east on McKinley Grove Road. Past the turnoff to Courtright Reservoir Road is the small Wishon Village store and private campground, where you can buy last-minute supplies, including campfire wood. The sign on the door of their saloon reads, "Monday Night Football—Bring your own finger food." Then, head up the hill to Courtright Reservoir; the ascent is gradual, beautiful, and well graded. Before you know it, you're there.

KEY INFORMATION

Trapper Springs Campground, Sierra National Forest
Kings River Ranger Station
P.O. Box 559
Prather, CA 93651

Operated by: Pacific Gas and Electric

Information: (559) 855-8321; www.r5.fs.fed.us/sierra

Open: June to October

Individual sites: 45

Each site has: Picnic table, fireplace

Registration: At entrance

Facilities: Water, vault toilets

Parking: At site

Fee: $15

Elevation: 8,200 feet

Restrictions:

Pets—On leash only

Fires—In fireplace

Vehicles—RVs up to 22 feet

To get there: from L.A., take I-5 north over the Tejon Pass to CA 99. Drive north on CA 99 past Bakersfield 104 miles to Fresno. Take CA 41 north to CA 168 and go northeast to Shaver Lake. From the town of Shaver Lake, turn east on Dinkey Creek Road and drive 12 miles to McKinley Grove Road. Drive 14 miles to Courtright Reservoir Road. Go left and proceed 12 miles up Courtright Reservoir Road to Trapper Springs Campground.

TWIN LAKES CAMPGROUND

Mammoth Lakes Area, Inyo National Forest

The Twin Lakes around the Twin Lakes Campground look like blue beans joined at the hip. A little bridge connects the two lakes, and folks in rental rowboats and canoes scoot underneath it. Grandfathers teach their grandchildren how to fish as a waterfall cascades down the cliff above the lakes.

The campground is both accessible and friendly. There are rustic cabins, a lodge, and a store. A few miles away, in the city of Mammoth Lakes, you'll find pizzerias, hardware stores, and a big wonderful Vons Supermarket on Old Mammoth Road. Twin Lakes Campground is a place to camp for a week; bring your family for the summer vacation.

The campsites sprawl around the two lakes and uphill across the road. If you find Twin Lakes Campground full, head a few hundred yards up the road to beautiful Coldwater Campground on Coldwater Creek. Or, head a mile or so up to Lake Mary Campground and Lake George Campground. All the sites are wonderful, but none is reservable. Phone the rangers to check on site availability and plan your trip so you arrive either in off-season or by Thursday for the weekend.

Head to the top of Coldwater Campground and walk a few hundred yards to the old Mammoth Consolidated Gold Mine on Mineral Hill. Here, you can see some of the old buildings from the mining

CAMPGROUND RATINGS

Beauty: ★★★★★
Site privacy: ★★★★
Site spaciousness: ★★★★★
Quiet: ★★★
Security: ★★★★★
Cleanliness/upkeep: ★★★★★

Twin Lakes Campground is a perfect place to spend summer vacation with the family.

towns and locations of the many bawdy houses and a saloon named The Temple of Folly (long-since destroyed). Walk around the old buildings and rusted machinery and imagine the men who sweated in the summer sun and froze in the winter, obsessed with gold. Climb up to the upper adit in the early morning for a view of Mount Banner and Mount Ritter.

Take the nice little hike to Emerald Lake. It's about a mile up the mountain. The trailhead and parking lot are next to the parking lot for the mine on Mineral Hill. Walk up by Coldwater Creek where there are lupine, monkeyflower, and fireweed. Bring a picnic and climb the rocks around the lake. Bring fishing gear as well. I watched one older woman reel in two decent trout while I ate my sandwich.

If you are ambitious, go around the left side of Emerald Lake. At the signed junction, go right to Gentian Meadow-Sky Meadows. Climb up by the inlet creek and reach tiny Gentian Meadow. Carry on up past a waterfall, and then, after a while you'll reach Sky Meadows. Look for paintbrush, corn lily, and elephant's heads among the grass. It's about 2.5 miles back down the hill.

Or, if you are truly ambitious, pick up the trail to Duck Pass (8.2 miles round-trip) back in the parking lot by the trailhead to Emerald Lake. Find the Duck Pass sign and start climbing. When you reach the entry sign for the John Muir Wilderness, bear right. Climb up through lodgepoles, pines, and hemlocks, and carry on past the trail to Arrowhead Lake, Skelton Lake, and Barney Lake. Next, you'll see alpine Duck Pass ahead, with all the high elevation flowers—columbine, gentian, and sorrel. Finally, traverse the pass and you'll see Duck Lake and pretty little Pika Lake on the left.

Back at Twin Lakes Campground, a nice stroll is around the shore to the falls. Access the trail behind campsite #24. You'll see a sign that says "Private/Public Road." Bear left and follow the trail that heads through the trees to the waterfall. Or, walk over to Tamarack Lodge. This graceful establishment was built in 1923. The clerk from the grocery store averred that Tamarack Lodge has the best food in Mammoth Lakes.

However, my wife and I ate *chez* campsite the last time I was at Twin Lakes. I boiled some quartered potatoes and set them aside. Then I fried up some onions, garlic, jalapeno peppers, and strips of chicken breast in the pot. After a bit, I returned the potatoes to the pot and stirred it all about. *Très délicieux* for a one-pot meal!

About 3:15 A.M., I heard a visitor. I jumped out of my sleeping bag and poked my head out of the tent. A three-foot bear was rifling through my cooler of soft drinks. I shouted, and the midget bear looked at me insolently and pawed on. I threw a pebble, and he ran over to a tree and climbed up a few feet. I retrieved my cooler. He gave me the evil eye and ran into the underbrush. The next morning he was rooting around in the big trash container down by the bridge. He glared at me and sauntered off combing garbage out of his whiskers.

To get there: from L.A., take I-5 north to CA 14. Go north to U.S. 395 near Inyokern. Go north on U.S. 395 for 123 miles to Bishop. Continue 37 miles north on U.S. 395 to Mammoth Lakes. From Mammoth Lakes, go west 3 miles on Lake Mary Road to the campground.

KEY INFORMATION

Twin Lakes Campground, Inyo National Forest
873 North Main Street
Bishop, CA 93514
Operated by: U.S. Forest Service
Information: (760) 924-5500; www.r5.fe.fed.us/inyo
Open: June to mid-October
Individual sites: 95
Each site has: Picnic table, fireplace
Registration: At entrance
Facilities: Water, flush toilets
Parking: At site
Fee: $13
Elevation: 8,600 feet
Restrictions:
  Pets—On leash only
  Fires—In fireplaces
  Vehicles—RVs up to 22 feet
  Other—Some handicapped-accessible sites

VERMILION CAMPGROUND

Lake Thomas A. Edison, Sierra National Forest

Vermilion Campground is superb tent camping and worth every bit of the terrifying but beautiful drive in over Kaiser Pass. Plan on at least a one-and-a-half-hour drive from Huntington Lake. Bring all provisions—only ice and a few sundries are available at Vermilion Valley Resort. Expect your automobile engine to hiccup a bit while climbing the 8,800-foot Kaiser Pass. (Buy premium gasoline for the climb; your car will thank you.) Turn on your lights, since the road is narrow, and remember, cars coming up have the right of way.

When you crest Kaiser Pass on the way to Vermillion, look out over the San Joaquin River Canyon and Kaiser Wilderness. John Muir wrote: "Westward, the general flank of the range is seen flowing sublimely away from the sharp summits, in smooth undulations; a sea of huge gray granite waves dotted with lakes and meadows, and fluted with stupendous canyons that grow steadily deeper as they recede into the distance."

At Vermillion, most sites are for tents only. This is no easy access for RVs, and most of the parking places are too short or steep for RVs. The pitches and picnic tables are a respectable distance away as well. At the campground you'll find sandy beaches and granite, pined points creating private coves and bays.

CAMPGROUND RATINGS

Beauty: ★★★★★
Site privacy: ★★★★★
Site spaciousness: ★★★★
Quiet: ★★★★
Security: ★★★★★
Cleanliness/upkeep: ★★★★★

Vermilion Campground proves that the best and most beautiful camping is usually the least accessible.

The swimming in Lake Edison was great. Granted, I was there in September, but you don't have to be a polar bear to enjoy jumping in and splashing around. Bring little rubber shoes for the children, so they can race through the shallows.

A friendly couple camping near my wife and I invited us to use their kayaks. We paddled east for about a half mile and beached on an island about 300 yards offshore. I swam and then lay on hot granite slabs and looked across at the snow fields on the mountains ringing the canyon. On a boat trolling by, I say a guy pull in at least a three-pound trout. What an incredible place!

The Vermilion Valley Resort runs a water ferry, which leaves the resort at 9:30 A.M. It drops you off to the east at the head of the lake. Where the fishing is spectacular. Some folks hike up the trail toward Mono Pass, and some just lie around and wait for the ferry to come pick them up at 4 P.M. The round-trip costs $15, and you can bring your dog for free.

You can also hike east of the campground about a mile to a respectable brook. There is a bridge about 300 yards north, or you can wade across and freeze your feet off. This water comes off a glacier for sure. A little farther, the trail splits. The left fork heads up Silver Pass to the John Muir Trail/Pacific Crest Trail. The right fork takes you 15 miles up to Mono Pass and down the other side to Rock Creek below Mammoth (using the ferry cuts miles off this hike).

The resort rents boats for about $50 a day. This is reasonable, especially when you consider the alternative of trailering a boat up over Kaiser Pass. The resort also has a little cafe and rents some pretty basic rooms. You can take a classy hot-spring soak in a deep tub at Mono Hot Springs.

Try to pick a campsite at Vermilion well away from the resort, since they run a generator until about 10 P.M. Wood is at a premium, and bundles are expensive at the resort store. Instead, bring a saw. East of the camp, along the trail to the brook, there are quite a few deadfalls. The sand around the pitches is fine and invasive. It's a good idea to bring along a bucket to dip your feet in before entering your tent. Bring a small brush to clean out the tent floor.

Be sure to check with rangers about the water before you arrive. The water at Vermilion is wonderful and spills out of a 400-foot artesian well, but, the day we left, an inspector came through and posted the water spigots with "not safe to drink" signs. I wished I'd brought a filter to purify the lake water, because the only other alternative was boiling it. Luckily, an hour later, the water scare turned out to be a false alarm.

If Vermilion is full, head back down the road a few miles to Mono Creek Campground. Or, try Mono Hot Springs, which has 26 sites. Since there is no dispersed camping in the area, the only other alternative is Jackass Meadow below the Florence Lake dam.

KEY INFORMATION

Vermilion Campground, Sierra National Forest
Pineridge Ranger Station
P.O. Box 559
Prather, CA 93651

Operated by: California Land Management

Information: (559) 855-5355 or (559) 297-0706; www.r5.fe.fed.us/sierra

Open: June to October

Individual sites: 11 tent sites, 20 sites for tents or RVs

Each site has: Picnic table, fireplace

Registration: At entrance; reserve by phone, (877) 444-6777, or online, www.reserveUSA.com

Facilities: Water, vault toilets

Parking: At or near site

Fee: $12; $8.65 nonrefundable reservation fee

Elevation: 7,000 feet

Restrictions:
  Pets—On leash only
  Fires—In fireplace
  Vehicles—RVs up to 16 feet
  Other—15 mph limit for boats on Lake Edison

To get there: from L.A., take I-5 north over the Tejon Pass to CA 99. Drive north on CA 99 past Bakersfield 104 miles to Fresno. Take CA 41 north to CA 168. Go northeast (right) to Shaver Lake. From Shaver Lake, head 20 miles north on CA 168 to Huntington Lake. From Lake Shore on Huntington Lake, take Kaiser Pass Road (FS 80) to Edison Lake Road at Mono Hot Springs. Continue 5 miles north to Vermilion Campground.

WHITE WOLF CAMPGROUND

Yosemite National Park

Yosemite National Park is heaven on earth. With the Mariposa Battalion, the first English-speaking party to see Yosemite Valley, was Lafayette Bunnell. He wrote: "The grandeur of the scene was softened by the haze that hung over the valley—light as gossamer—and by the clouds which partially dimmed the higher cliffs and mountains. This obscurity of vision merely increased the awe with which I beheld it, and as I looked, a peculiar exalted sensation seemed to fill my whole being, and I found my eyes in tears with emotion."

The Yosemite Native Americans, the original inhabitants, loved the valley too, but the arrival of forty-niners ended their resiliency. By 1852, Chief Tenaya of the Yosemites, his tribe decimated, was stoned to death by some raiding Mono Native Americans. Soon after, August T. Dowd, a miner hunting in the valley, saw a tree bigger than he'd ever seen before. He told his friends about it, and the tourists began flooding in. Yosemite Valley became a mecca to the world.

Now, four-hour traffic jams in Yosemite Valley are common, and the campgrounds are constantly booked. Avoid Yosemite Valley, and explore the rest of the park instead. Come in from the east over the Tioga Pass off U.S. 395 or from the west on CA 120. Shun CA 41, and don't get stuck in the Wawona Tunnel.

CAMPGROUND RATINGS

Beauty: ★★★★★
Site privacy: ★★★★★
Site spaciousness: ★★★★★
Quiet: ★★★★★
Security: ★★★★★
Cleanliness/upkeep: ★★★★★

White Wolf Campground is the only campground in Yosemite National Park worth squeezing into.

However, you should see Tuolumne Meadows and camp in White Wolf Campground. John Muir eloquently described the Tioga Pass area: "From garden to garden, ridge to ridge, I drifted enchanted, now on my knees gazing into the face of a daisy, now climbing again and again among the purple and azure flowers of the hemlocks, now down into the treasuries of the snow, or gazing far over domes and peaks, lakes and woods, and the billowy glaciated fields of the upper Tuolumne. In

the midst of such beauty, pierced with its rays, one's body is all one tingling palate. Who wouldn't be a mountaineer! Up here all the world's prizes seem nothing."

White Wolf Campground is full of tiny meadows and stands of lodgepole pine, and the Middle Tuolumne River flows through the campground. The sites are set among the pines and granite boulders. The campground is constructed beautifully; each loop seems miles away from the others. The arrangement of the tables and sites create a sense of spaciousness. The facilities are clean and well tended. This is slow, elegant camping.

Only the little bear wandering around camp caused a little nervousness. Obviously he was a special bear because he had little colored tags in his ears. Our neighbor shook a towel at the little bear, and he decamped, at least for that day. Of course, we were careful to put away our coolers even if we were only leaving camp for a moment. Bears get a record for raiding campers, and the rangers are forced to take steps. We didn't want that to happen to the little bear with tags in his ears.

We hiked up to Hardin Lake and sat under the pines reading, John Muir. Muir cavorted through these mountains, wearing a great coat, and carried all his gear in his pockets. At night, he lay down in the same great coat and slept. Those old-timers were real men! Take John A. "Snowshoe" Thompson, for example. Every winter from 1856 to 1876, Thompson carried the U.S. mail alone across the Sierra. Traveling on skis (called snowshoes in those days), Thompson carried a 100-pound pack and made the 180-mile round-trip in five days. His diet consisted of beef jerky and crackers, and he drank snow. He didn't carry a blanket or wear an overcoat.

At night, Thompson would find a tree stump. After setting fire to the stump, he'd cut some fir boughs for a bed. With his feet to the fire, he'd sleep through the worst blizzards. If he was caught outside camp in a bad blizzard, he just stood on a rock and danced a jig to stay warm.

Today, camping life is a little easier. Still, remember to get supplies in the western flatlands or in Mammoth Lakes on your way in from the east. Only ice, beer, and soda are available in Tuolumne Meadows, Crane Flat, and White Wolf Lodge near White Wolf Campground (in the summer months only).

KEY INFORMATION

White Wolf Campground
Yosemite National Park
P.O. Box 577
Yosemite, CA 95389

Operated by: National Park Service

Information: (209) 372-8502; www.nps.gov/yose; for recorded information, call (209) 372-0200

Open: June to September

Individual sites: 74

Each site has: Picnic table, fireplace

Registration: At entrance; reserve by phone, (800) 436-7275, or online, www.reservations.nps.gov

Facilities: Water, flush toilets, food storage lockers

Parking: At site

Fee: $12

Elevation: 8,000 feet

Restrictions:

Pets—On leash only

Fires—In fireplace

Vehicles—RVs up to 27 feet

To get there: from L.A., take I-5 north to CA 14. Head north to U.S. 395 near Inyokern. Go north on U.S. 395 for 123 miles to Bishop. Continue north on U.S. 395 for 57 miles to CA 120 (Tioga Pass Road). Go west 43 miles to White Wolf Road on the right. The White Wolf Campground is about a mile down that road.

WISHON CAMPGROUND

Camp Wishon, Sequoia National Forest

As you leave the little town of Spring-dale and head east toward Camp Wishon, you feel as if you're leaving civilization behind. All the stores and gas stations have a last-chance look, and the road signs anticipate the high mountain passes ahead—"Chains may be required" or "No night plowing." The only vehicles on the road are big pickups with four-wheel drive as CA 190 begins to climb, following the turns of the Middle Fork Tule River. The roadside scenery strips down to big rocks and chaparral. There are two picnic areas, then the huge flume carrying water down to the power plant below, and then the turnoff north to the campground, up Wishon Drive, along the North Fork of the Middle Fork Tule River.

Wishon Drive is steep and narrow and winds along a steep pitch down to the river. You'll find good fishing here. In the spring, the big pickups are parked at the turnouts, and their drivers are down below fishing for trout. Here, the snow level can come down to 3,000 feet. Think about chains for the ride down if you hit bad weather. Then, suddenly, you're out of the chaparral and into the Yellow Pine Belt with the pines, firs, big-leaf maple, oaks, cedars, and lilac. The road dips into a beautiful, flat canyon where you'll see the campground—more of a forested glade—by the river, with its alders and cottonwood.

CAMPGROUND RATINGS

Beauty: ★★★★★
Site privacy: ★★★★
Site spaciousness: ★★★★
Quiet: ★★★★
Security: ★★★★★
Cleanliness/upkeep: ★★★★

Wishon Campground offers good fishing, good hiking, and a long camping season.

It was raining heavily the day we arrived at Wishon, and my wife fell in love with the place. The campsites are all spacious and private. There's a Ranger Station at the gate. We saw big, happy, wet men in rain gear stoking fires to keep warm, and you knew they had spent the morning fishing. The campground location and layout, and the feeling you get when you arrive make you want to pull up, relax, and stay for a couple days. At 4,000 feet, it will snow in late spring. We wanted it to,

so we could stay longer. There was enough downed wood around our campsite to keep us warm around the fire that night. (Bring charcoal fire starter along to get wet wood going easily for your camp fire.)

I pitched the tent away from the stream to avoid the downward current of cold air that blows down the Sierras at night. It's always a good idea, too, if you're sleeping outside to point your feet into the wind; you'll stay a lot warmer.

The first thing we heard in the morning were the birds. It all began with the noisy black-headed grosbeak and its cheery rising and falling notes. It has a rust-colored body with a black head and black and white wings. With its very thick beak, you'd think it was a seed eater, but it also eats buds and insects in the upper canopy of trees. We saw the mountain chickadee and heard its sad song—three slow notes, two high tones, and one lower. It's a small bird with a gray body and black and white stripes on its head. Another was the dark-eyed junco, a small gray bird with a dark head.

We saw many western gray squirrels who survive the winter on buried caches of acorns or pine seeds. They remember and dig down through the snow to dinner. If a squirrel dies, the acorns often germinate, which is why oak trees tend to grow in clumps. A botanist friend of mine also offered another explanation for clumped oaks—the regeneration of sprouts from a single clump after a fire.

During the day, the wind kicked up from west to east. I have read that this is caused by air heating up more rapidly in the desert, which makes it rise, which draws air from the coast over the top of the Sierra Nevada. As it reaches higher elevations and narrower canyons, the wind moves faster as it ascends (the chimney effect) to the summit where it descends into the Owens Valley and becomes heated by compression. So, the daily air flow in the Sierras is uphill in the west and downhill in the east during the day. At night, of course, cold air spills down the mountains on both sides.

We hiked as far as the weather would allow along a trail going northeast out of camp along the river that heads to Mountain Home State Forest and the campgrounds there—Balch, Hedrick Pond, Frazier Mill, and Shake Camp. This is lovely country.

KEY INFORMATION

**Wishon Campground,
  Sequoia National Forest**
Tule River Ranger District
32588 Highway190
Springville, CA 932657

Operated by: U.S. Forest Service

Information: (559) 784-1500 or (559) 539-2607; www.r5.fs.fed.us/sequoia

Open: All year

Individual sites: 10 sites for tents only, 26 sites for tents or RVs

Each site has: Picnic table, fireplace

Registration: At entrance; reserve by phone, (877) 444-6777, or online, www.reserveUSA.com

Facilities: Water, vault toilets

Parking: At site

Fee: $12; $8.65 nonrefundable reservation fee

Elevation: 4,000 feet

Restrictions:
  Pets—On leash only
  Fires—In fireplaces
  Vehicles—RVs up to 22 feet

To get there: from L.A., take I-5 north over the Tejon Pass to CA 99. Drive north on CA 99 past Bakersfield. Take CA 65 north to Porterville. From Porterville drive 25 miles east on CA 190. Turn north (left) on Wishon Drive and go 3.5 miles. There's a ranger station on the right and a few campsites. The main campground is farther to the right over a bridge and then left.

SOUTHERN CALIFORNIA

THE SOUTHERN SIERRAS

DARK CANYON CAMPGROUND

Pine Grove, San Bernardino National Forest

I drove through Idyllwild in a mist so thick the neon lights of the cute little mountain town could only blush through the fog. I found a place to park and drifted along a sidewalk until I ran right into a Mt. San Jacinto State Park ranger who said this fog never happens this time of year. It was June 15th; it was supposed to be sunny and at least 80°F.

Back on CA 243, I leaned out the window and navigated by the stripes down the middle of the highway until Forest Service Road 4S02 split off to the right, and I could reckon the road by aiming for the gap in the pines. After traveling down the narrowing road and across a stream, I was at Dark Canyon Campground, one of the most charming campgrounds in the very charming Idyllwild area of the San Bernardinos.

Upon arrival, it took me a minimal amount of time to find the perfect campsite down by the stream that runs through the canyon. The water is cold and runs clear around granite boulders through pools with clean sand bottoms. In this area, and most parts of the San Bernardino National Forest, water is at a premium.

The 21 campsites in Dark Canyon are perfect for tent camping. The fireplaces and picnic tables for some of the sites are a 15-yard walk away from the parking lot (ample enough for an RV, however). Five sites are located down by the stream and

CAMPGROUND RATINGS

Beauty: ★★★★★
Site privacy: ★★★★
Site spaciousness: ★★★★
Quiet: ★★★★★
Security: ★★★★★
Cleanliness/upkeep: ★★★★★

Dark Canyon Campground is a heartbreaker—so beautiful and so near Los Angeles. Reserve!

the rest are up in the pines above the campground.

Shortly after I arrived, it started snowing, and my hike around the canyon was screened through the hard-driving sleet and wet snow. What I saw were pines; Dark Canyon is right on the line between north-facing Upper Chaparral and the higher Yellow Pine Forest. Both of these areas are packed with pines—Coulter pine, white fir, incense cedar, sugar and yellow pine. Down by the stream, you'll see riparian trees like alder, willow, and black cottonwood.

I hiked a mile or so up the dirt road to the trailhead that heads east into Mt. San Jacinto State Park to Deer Springs. By this time, it was sleeting harder, so I endeavored to collect some dry wood and light a fire in my fireplace. Fortunately, I had a can of charcoal lighter fluid, which, when combined with a little dry paper and a modest amount of kindling, will start up just about any campground wood. I know lighter fluid doesn't sound kosher to the former Boy Scout planning a camping trip at home in the living room, but, when everyone is blowing and fanning wet pine needles and wet wood, this petroleum distillate cheater can make you look like a hero. On the other hand, hardware stores also sell a small hatchet-sized splitter, which does a good job chopping wood into more easily lit kindling if you can't handle the humiliation of the tenderfoot charcoal fluid.

Dark Canyon is very popular. The campground hostess told me it usually fills up early Friday afternoon for the weekends. On big weekends, she recommended arriving on Thursday. It's a great idea to make a reservation.

If you decide not to reserve, look for you will the sign on FS 4S02 informing you if Dark Canyon Campground and its two sister campgrounds, Fern Basin and Marion Mountain, are full. If so, drive to Idyllwild and go to the Ranger Station on the left as you enter town. They will direct you to dispersed camping areas. Some of these are "yellow post" areas, which means you can have a fire in the metal fire ring. Other areas require a fire permit, which will be issued at the station if fire conditions allow it.

Other alternatives include the two Mt. San Jacinto State Park campgrounds. Idyllwild Campground is right smack in town by the Mt. San Jacinto State Park Ranger Station. It is clean (flush toilets and showers), safe, and especially wonderful on Sunday morning when you feel like walking 100 yards to Idyllwild for brunch and the Sunday paper. Many of Idyllwild's sites are for tents only, which makes it especially friendly. Stone Creek is out of town and a little more primitive.

The last time I visited, Stone Creek Campground was closed. I asked a particularly crusty ranger why. "Plague," he said. "My God, I guess I don't want to camp there!" I whined. "Oh, hell!" he said. "We're just going to dust all the squirrels down for fleas, and that's that." He'd be damned if he ever heard of anybody getting the plague from squirrels and allowed that it was no reason to give up camping. "Just don't feed the little beggars corn chips and you'll be all right," he assured me.

To get there: from L.A., drive east on I-10 to Banning. Take CA 243 south 22 miles toward Idyllwild. Turn left on FS 4S02 and go another 3 miles to the campground.

KEY INFORMATION

Dark Canyon Campground, San Bernardino National Forest

San Jacinto Ranger District
P.O. Box 518, 54270 Pinecrest
Idyllwild, CA 92549

Operated by: U.S. Forest Service

Information: (909) 659-2117; www.r5.fs.fed.us/ sanbernadino

Open: May to mid-October

Individual sites: 16

Each site has: Fire pit, picnic table

Registration: At entrance; reserve by phone, (877) 444-6777, or online, www.reserveUSA.com

Facilities: Water, vault toilets

Parking: Within 20 yards of sites

Fee: $12, $5 extra vehicle fee; $8.65 nonrefundable reservation fee

Elevation: 5,800 feet

Restrictions:

Pets—On leash only

Fires—In fire pit

Vehicles—No RVs over 22 feet

Other—Road in is very narrow; maximum of 8 people per site

DOANE VALLEY CAMPGROUND

Palomar Mountain State Park

Palomar means "place of the pigeons," and Palomar Mountain feels so Mediterranean, you'll think you're in Italy. There's a sense of tradition and civilization on the mountain. Maybe that feeling comes from the fact that Native Americans gathered acorns here long ago, or drifts down from the incredible hand-crafted observatory on the summit, or maybe it stems from the sense of awe observatory visitors get when they realize we live in but a tiny part of the universe. Anyway, Palomar Mountain State Park Campground offers good tent camping and great family camping.

Built by the Civilian Conservation Corps in the 1930s (when folks tent camped and cars were tiny Fords), the campsites are styled in stone and set under huge trees. The toilets are clean, and the hot showers cost a few quarters. The park headquarters is back up the road on the way in and, when I was there, was staffed by a helpful lady ranger who looked like a young Elke Sommer. Included in the park area is a Christian Conference Center and a School Camp, both infested with boisterous junior high schoolers. If you tire of camp grub, at the intersection of County Road S6 and S7, you'll find Mother's Kitchen Restaurant, which serves good food.

Near the campground is Doane's Pond, a cute pond with picnic tables set around it under ramadas, since it gets hot here in the

CAMPGROUND RATINGS

Beauty: ★★★
Site privacy: ★★★★
Site spaciousness: ★★★
Quiet: ★★★
Security: ★★★★★
Cleanliness/upkeep: ★★★★

Camp at Doane Valley Campground to see the stars at Palomar Observatory, eat at Mother's Kitchen Restaurant, and bring home 10 pounds of gems.

summer. On the road in, you'll see a sign threatening a $500 fine for miscreants throwing snowballs at cars or people, so you know snow drifts up a bit here in the winter. I think the best time to visit is in the spring or fall. But, the Palomar Observatory qualifies the mountain as a wonderful place to visit year-round. I think it's easier to view ourselves as creatures of the larger universe when camping than when home watching television. Buy the star map in the observatory gift

shop and go out in the meadow by Doane's Pond at night. Imagine how the ancients must have felt in a world lit only by starlight and fire.

I followed a group of junior high schoolers and heard their teacher try to pique the loutish pupils' interest in the observatory. It really is amazing. The dome weighs 1,000 tons and is so well engineered that it can be moved by hand. The telescope, which weighs 750 tons, can also be moved by the touch of a finger. The glass disk at the heart of the telescope was ground and polished to the two-millionth part of an inch. Incredible!

It wasn't hard to spot the band-tailed pigeon that gives Palomar Mountain its name. The band-tail is not your ordinary "rat with wings" pigeon cadging food at the local patio restaurant, but a lovely bird with a yellow bill, green nape, and white neck band. It's call is a low-pitched, owl-like "coo-coo."

Like the band-tail, the acorn woodpecker eats acorns. It goes around storing them by the thousands in specially drilled holes—each containing a single acorn—in dead trees, telephone poles, fence posts, and even the sides of buildings. Its diligence is equaled only by the gray squirrel, who hides acorns in underground caches and later smells them out. Acorns are a big industry on the mountain.

The Luiseno Native Americans, who also collected acorns on Palomar, ate manzanita berries, choke cherries, and toyon berries. For salad and veggies, they ate lily bulbs, tree mushrooms, yucca blossoms, sage shoots, wild mustard, clover, and celery. In season, they relished watercress, lamb's quarter, and Indian lettuce. Palomar is a bountiful mountain.

If you don't find a site at Doane Valley Campground (reserve ahead for weekends!), there are two Forest Service Camps up the road to the observatory. At wide-open Observatory Campground there are huge oaks and views of the ridges. Just a quarter-mile up is Fry Creek Campground, a nice campground in the woods that favors tent campers because the road in is too narrow for RVs or trailers.

A good side trip from Palomar is to Gems of Pala, just down the road toward I-15. It's open Thursday through Sunday 10 A.M.–4 P.M. For a fee, you get to dig in one of the world's foremost tourmaline locations. Bring a garden shovel, a spray bottle, and an eighth-of-an-inch mesh screen about one foot by two feet. You get to take home up to ten pounds of pink, blue, green, black, and watermelon tourmaline. Call Gems of Pala at (619) 742-1356 for information.

To get there: from L.A., drive east on I-10. Take I-15 south to the intersection with CA 76. Drive east 21 miles to County Road S-6. Go north (left) 6.8 miles, then left on County Road S-7 3 miles to the campground.

KEY INFORMATION

Doane Valley Campground
Palomar Mountain State Park
19952 State Park Road
Palomar Mountain, CA 92060

Operated by: California Department of Parks and Recreation

Information: (760) 742-3462; http://parks.ca.gov; for information on neighboring Cleveland National Forest call the Palomar Ranger District at (760) 788-0250

Open: All year

Individual sites: 21 for tents only, 10 for RVs

Each site has: Fireplace, picnic table

Registration: At entrance; reserve by phone, (800) 444-7275, or online, www.reservamerica.com

Facilities: Water, flush toilets, coin-operated, hot showers

Parking: Near site

Fee: $15 Sunday–Thursday; $17 Friday and Saturday; $8.65 nonrefundable reservation fee

Elevation: 4,700 feet

Restrictions:

Pets—On leash only; $1 fee; not allowed on trails

Fires—In fireplace

Vehicles—RVs up to 27 feet

HANNA FLAT CAMPGROUND

Fawnskin, San Bernardino National Forest

"Abandon hope all ye who enter here" is a good motto for campers coming to Big Bear Lake on holiday weekends, but during mid week or off-season, the north shore is downright civilized. It's a beautiful place, and the rangers and civilians are genuinely friendly.

Hanna Flat Campground features good tent camping. The sites are set in stands of Jeffrey pine and spaced nicely to allow vistas of pine-covered and rocky hills with the blue-sky, big-country look. Manzanita grows under the pines, and there's a mild riparian community by the cut along the campground. Best of all, the sites are engineered to give campers maximum privacy and space. Each site has an abundance of flat, spongy, and pine-needled ground.

Hanna Flat Campground is run by Alpine Camping Services, a private company, and they do a good job. At Hanna Flat they are represented by a Grizzly Adams–type fellow in rawhide boots and by his dad back at the Camp Host trailer. There are clean pit and flush toilets.

The few miles of dirt road coming in discourages most RVers, who prefer a site down by the lake in parks with hookups. In the nearby village of Fawnskin, you'll find a little grocery store and two homespun eateries. For serious shopping go around the lake to Big Bear City. There's a Thrifty as big as an aircraft carrier and more banks than you can shake a stick at.

CAMPGROUND RATINGS

Beauty: ★★★★
Site privacy: ★★★★★
Site spaciousness: ★★★★★
Quiet: ★★★★★
Security: ★★★★★
Cleanliness/upkeep: ★★★★

Hanna Flat Campground is "Big Sky" country, with fishing, biking, and hiking. But don't get caught alive here on big holidays.

Lake access from Hanna Flat Campground begins in Fawnskin's Dana Point Marina, which has a bait shop, picnic tables, a lake beach, and toilets. A sign announces roosting bald eagles from November to March. Fawnskin is charming. I loved all the rustic wood cottages.

More lake access lies below Serrano Camground, a few miles east of Fawnskin. There's a marina that rents boats and bicycles, an observatory, a paved hiking and biking path, and Meadow's Edge Picnic Ground,

with all the amenities and a nice lake beach. The observatory dome is out on the water at the end of a dock, since water cuts down on image distortion. Noted for its study of the sun, the observatory is open to visitors on Saturday, from 4–6 P.M., between July 4th and Labor Day.

Just past Serrano Campground is the Big Bear Ranger Station, where you can get maps of all the hiking trails. Big Bear offers good hiking and is a world-renowned mountain biking center. Snow Summit, a snow-ski resort, utilizes its chairlifts in the summer to carry mountain bikers to the top of the mountain, at 8,200 feet, where there are 60 miles of trails accessible. The real fanatics go down Snow Summit's single-track downhills about 90 mph.

Back at the Hanna Flat Campground, you'll find two fun hikes; one heads out from site #51 to Grout Bay, and the other goes from site #25 north and back along the road. The trail to Grout Bay is an 8-mile round-trip with lovely views of the lake from the plateau. Look for eagles on the tops of dead trees. From this trail, you can also access the trail to Gray's Peak. The trail is a bit rough as you near the summit.

The second hike takes you north to the beaver dams on Holcomb Creek. Here, beavers live in dens in caves along the water's edge. To more easily access to the dams, drive your car out of the campground, turn left on the dirt road you came in on (FS 3N14), and go a mile or so to a parking lot on the right before Holcomb Creek. Find the Pacific Crest Trail just north across the creek and to the left of FS 3N14. Follow the trail west about a mile to see the beaver dams. Look for wildflowers along the way. I was able to identify wild rose, lupine, Indian paintbrush, and scarlet bugler.

Look at the mountains around Big Bear Lake and imagine—this was once the bottom of the ocean! Of course, that was about 600 million years ago. Then, 60 million years ago, the earth's plates ground together and pushed the ocean floor up to make the San Bernardinos.

The Big Bear Lake area can get crowded, so time your visits for maximum enjoyment. As you drive up the mountains to Big Bear, remember the area's first tourists, who rode two days on burros up to the Bear Valley Hotel

On the way home, drive the Rim of the World Highway (CA 38) to Redlands. Built in 1915, this road provided the first automobile access to Big Bear (no more burros!). The scenery is sensational.

To get there: from L.A., go east on I-10, almost to San Bernardino. Then take CA 30 north to CA 330. About 35 miles later, you will arrive at the Big Bear Lake dam. Go left on CA 38 for 4 miles to Fawnskin. Turn left on Rim of the World Road. It becomes FS 3N14. Follow this dirt road a couple miles to Hanna Flat Campground on the left.

KEY INFORMATION

Hanna Flat Campground, San Bernardino National Forest Big Bear Discovery Center
P.O. Box 66
North Shore Drive, CA 38
Fawnskin, CA 92333

Operated by: California Land Management

Information: 909-383-5588
www.r5.fs.fed.us/sanbernadino

Open: April to October (phone ahead)

Individual sites: 88

Each site has: Picnic table, fire ring

Registration: At entrance (or with host); reserve by phone, (877) 444-6777, or online, www.reserveUSA.com

Facilities: Water, flush toilets

Parking: At site

Fee: $15; $8.65 nonrefundable reservation fee

Elevation: 7,000 feet

Restrictions:

Pets—On leash only

Fires—In fire ring

Vehicles—RVs up to 30 feet long

HEART BAR CAMPGROUND

Aspen Grove, San Bernardino National Forest

Drive up to Big Bear on CA 330 and you feel like a rat in a maze. The road zips up through carnival-ride corners shouldered with impenetrable chaparral. Oncoming traffic appears out of nowhere. Suddenly, behind you, there's a string of impatient cars. You pull over, and they fly by in a flash of waxed paint and chrome.

You'll find a different scene on old CA 38, Rim of the World Scenic Highway. Drive out of Big Bear into a sea of granite and lodgepole pine and feast your eyes on "Greyback" himself, San Gorgonio Mountain at 11,502 feet (named for a very, very obscure Christian martyr). Come up from the bottom, from Redlands down in the desert, and suddenly you are in subalpine (boreal) forests of lodgepole pine twisted by the storms. The chaparral is high-altitude chaparral. There's manzanita, bush chinquapin, snowbrush, and all the alpine wildflowers. It's incredible! One moment you're driving through the mess of the city of San Bernardino, and the next you're in the splendor of the San Gorgonio Wilderness.

Heart Bar Campground is right in the belly of the beast. Why Heart Bar? It's a beautiful name. Here, in an area settled by pioneer Mormans, cattle herds were summered up in the meadows by the headwaters of the Santa Ana River. One of the local brands was the Heart Bar, a heart with a bar beneath it.

CAMPGROUND RATINGS

Beauty: ★★★★
Site privacy: ★★★★
Site spaciousness: ★★★★
Quiet: ★★★★★
Security: ★★★★
Cleanliness/upkeep: ★★★★★

Heart Bar Campground is in the heart of San Gorgonio Wilderness. This is real mountain camping right near Los Angeles. Reserve for big holidays.

I love this campground. It's big and shaded, but it feels wide open. The meadow is green and bright in the sunlight. The pitches are clean and softened by pine needles. The sites are nicely spaced. And, the camground is not nearly as heavily used as nearby South Fork Campground, bunched along Lost Creek, or Barton Flats down below.

There is great hiking from the campground, stream fishing down by the South Fork Campground, and great lake fishing a short shot up at Big Bear Lake. At Big Bear, you can buy anything a body could need from big chain stores and little antique joints. Or, the other way, in Angelus Oaks, there's a general store as well as the Oaks Restaurant and El Mexicano Restaurant. You can also go farther and then left along Mill Creek to Forest Falls where there is another general store.

For an easily accessed hike, head south a few hundred yards from Heart Bar Campground and connect with a trail that goes east to the headwaters of the Santa Ana River or west along its banks to South Fork Campground. Up here, the Santa Ana is a beautiful little stream flowing through meadows and forests of black oak, fir, and Jeffrey and ponderosa pine. Formed from natural springs and snowmelt, the Santa Ana River looks incredibly beautiful up here, yet hideously ugly down in Orange County in its concrete channel.

Or, hike up Wildhorse Creek. Walk out to the main road and go left. About 300 yards along you'll see a signed turnoff to the Wildhorse Trail on the right. Follow the dirt road up to a parking lot. The trail leaves from here. At first, it is an old road up through pines and juniper. Then it winds up a series of chaparral-covered ridges before going down into Wildhorse Creek Canyon. Walk about a mile and find Wildhorse Creek Trail Camp. Right now, you are about three-and-a-half miles out.

An ambitious hiker could continue on and climb Sugar Loaf Mountain. Sugar Loaf has an elevation of about 9,952 feet and is a big lump on the divide between Big Bear country and the Santa Ana River Canyon. The best way is to hike up the saddle east of Sugar Loaf, then follow the trail along the ridgetop to the summit. I kept hearing about a famous, rare black butterfly and looked in vain for it when I was last there in September.

Another fun hike from Heart Bar Campground is to Aspen Grove. Go in the fall when the leaves are golden yellow. Head out of the campground to FS 1N02 (the road you drove in on). Turn right and walk about a mile to a fork in the road. Go right again and walk to a small parking lot near the signed trailhead for Aspen Grove Trail. Follow the old dirt road southeast to Fish Creek. Cross the creek and enjoy the aspens—or what's left of them. Apparently, the California golden beaver enjoys them, too. A fellow hiker said that this particular beaver is not a San Bernardino native, but was introduced by Forest Service wildlife experts who had not counted on the beaver's sudden passion for eating aspen.

Check out the dispersed camping in the area for future trips. Stop at the Mill Creek Ranger Station on CA 38 near the burg of Mentone. You'll need a wilderness permit for ambitious hiking anyway. Ask the ranger to show you where dispersed camping is allowed and where the yellow-post sites are. There is spectacular tent camping in the San Gorgonio area, and much of it is outside the organized campgrounds.

KEY INFORMATION

Heart Bar Campground, San Bernardino National Forest
San Gorgonio Ranger District
34701 Mill Creek Road
Mentone, CA 92359

Operated by: U.S. Forest Service

Information: (909) 794-1123; www.r5.fs.fed.us/ sanbernardino

Open: All year (phone ahead)

Individual sites: 94

Each site has: Picnic table, fireplace

Registration: At entrance (or with host); reserve by phone, (877) 444-6777, or online, www.reserveUSA.com

Facilities: Water, vault toilets

Parking: At site

Fee: $10–20; no fee for hiking, but auto touring costs $5 per day or $30 annually

Elevation: 7,000 feet

Restrictions:

  Pets—On leash only

  Fires—In fireplaces

  Vehicles—RVs up to 50 feet long

  Other—Get a wilderness permit from Mill Creek Ranger Station

To get there: from L.A., go east on I-10 to Redlands past San Bernardino. Then take CA 38 east 33 miles to FS 1N02 and go right. The campground entrance is immediately on your right.

LAGUNA CAMPGROUND

Mount Laguna, Cleveland National Forest

Laguna Campground offers some of the best camping in Southern California and the cheekiest ground squirrels and jays in the West. Hardly had my wife and I arrived at an incredible campsite on the edge of a yellow-flowered meadow stretching away to islands of pine against a cerulean blue sky, when a larcenous Stellar's jay swooped down on the picnic table and tried to make off with a particularly shiny spoon. Next, the California ground squirrels moved in for a package of corn chips on top of the cooler. I stomped my feet and threw gravel. They scurried a few feet away, rolled defiantly in the dust, and rose to attack the corn chips again. Then, I heard a shrill shreik and the varmits scattered at the sight of a red-tailed hawk circling above.

Maintained by the Laguna Mountain Volunteer Association, Laguna Campground is clean and well run. There's a feeling of serenity and order. The little community of Laguna with its stores, churches, fire department, restaurants, and rental cabins reflects the pride of its residents. This is a very special place.

The campground is set in a meadow in a stand of Jeffrey pines, almost indistinguishable from ponderosa pines save the vanilla scent of their bark. Put your nose right up to the tree and take a whiff. Also, the bark on the Jeffrey tends toward narrow ridges while ponderosa bark grows in large, flat

CAMPGROUND RATINGS

Beauty: ★★★★★
Site privacy: ★★★★
Site spaciousness: ★★★★
Quiet: ★★★★★
Security: ★★★★★
Cleanliness/upkeep: ★★★★★

Laguna Campground is clean, well run, and near the proud community of Laguna. Come for alpine meadows all year.

plates. Roll the cones from a Jeffrey between your hands, and the spines won't prick—they are turned under. Ponderosa spines stick out.

Native Americans used the roots of Jeffrey Pines to make baskets. They waited until the trees flowered and the roots were sufficiently tough. Then, they dug up the roots, cleaned, and slow cooked them. Afterwards, the roots were split and scraped until soft and pliable enough to weave.

I met a German naturalist camping a few sites over

who gave me the rundown on the squirrels. They are supposed to eat seeds, herbaceous vegetation, and acorns, but prefer to hang around campgrounds and eat corn chips. They hibernate in the winter; when spring comes, they have some catch-up eating to do. According to the naturalist, the shrill squeak I heard when the hawk cruised overhead was from the oldest squirrel in the colony. Apparently, the squirrel who sounds the alarm has the greatest chance of being picked off by the hawk. So, the oldest squirrel protects his own offspring, and the band, by sounding the alarm and offering himself as the victim if need be. Pretty brave stuff for the little guy.

In the meadow by the campground is Little Laguna Lake. Little more than a wallow, it is still home to many water fowl and loudly croaking frogs. A kopje (stand of rocks in a meadow) nearby is a convenient place to sit and watch the wildlife through binoculars. The meadow was carpeted with tiny sunflowers, tidy tips, Achilles's fern, and the edible miner's lettuce when I visited in June.

We picked up a trail to Big Laguna Lake to the south of the campground. The trail meanders for about a mile across meadows and along the edge of the pined hummocks that beg for picnickers. Big Laguna Lake, which is only a lake indeed in the spring and summer of wet years, was big and beautiful on our visit. From the lake, the mostly flat trail turns north and connects with Noble Canyon Trail and Pine Creek Road.

If you want a desert view, trade the pines of Laguna for the oaks of Burnt Rancheria Campground a few miles south and also run by the Laguna Mountain Volunteer Society.

Laguna Campground is open all year (Burnt Rancheria is open May to October), but I think spring is the best time to visit. In winter, there's snow and snow sports, but half of San Diego flocks here on wintry weekends. Summers get a bit hot and dusty. Both campgrounds are popular, so plan on getting there Friday by noon if you don't have a reservation.

While visiting, run down to Tecate, Mexico (a half hour to the south). Or, take I-8 to Anza-Borrego Desert State Park or the Sunrise Highway north to Julian to fish in Lake Cuyamaca. There is a lot to do around here. Go horseback riding or mountain biking. Stargaze from the night-sky observatories at the south end of the recreation area. This is a wonderful part of Southern California.

To get there: from San Diego, drive 50 miles east on I-8 to the Laguna Junction exit. Drive 11 miles north on Sunrise Highway to Mt. Laguna, then 2.5 miles farther north to the signed entrance on the left marked "Laguna/El Prado." Laguna is the campground you want. El Prado is the nearby group campground.

KEY INFORMATION

Laguna Campground, Cleveland National Forest Descanso Ranger District 3348 Alpine Boulevard Alpine, CA 91901

Operated by: U.S. Forest Service

Information: Ranger Office, (619) 445-6235 or (619) 473-8824 (Monday–Friday, 8 A.M.–4:30 P.M.); Visitors Center, (619) 473-8547 (Friday–Sunday, May through September); www.r5.fs.fed.us/cleveland

Open: Year round

Individual sites: 30 exclusively for tents; 103 total

Each site has: Picnic table, fireplace

Registration: At entrance; reserve by phone, (877) 444-6777, or online, www.reserveUSA.com

Facilities: Water, vault toilets, showers

Parking: Near site

Fee: $13; $8.65 nonrefundable reservation fee

Elevation: 5,800 feet

Restrictions:

Pets—On leash only; must stay in tent or vehicle overnight

Fires—In fireplace

Vehicles—RVs (maximum 25 feet), trailers

MARION MOUNTAIN CAMPGROUND

San Jacinto, San Bernardino National Forest

From L.A., the ride to Marion Mountain Campground on I-10 through "The Inland Empire" (a.k.a. "Land of Swirling Gases") is, at best, horrifying. Persevere, though, and head up CA 243 from Banning, and, in a few short minutes, you'll be in a different world. You'll come up out of the chaparral into the pines and peaks. What a contrast!

Marion Mountain Campground is as sunny and airy as nearby Dark Canyon Campground is dark and safe, down under sheltering trees. Between the two, you'll see the entire spectrum of good San Jacinto tent camping.

The access road to Marion Mountain Campground from CA 243 is narrow and winding. This cuts down on the trailers and RVs. The site parking spaces are short—about 15 feet tops. The picnic tables and fireplaces are down in the trees away from the parking area. All this discourages RVers and gives an edge to tent campers.

The water from a spring above the campground is good. Let the tap run for a moment to clear any sediment if the campground has been lightly used. All the facilities are well maintained. The pit toilet bathrooms are surprisingly clean and tiled on the floors and walls. I wanted to stay for a week.

When you first arrive at Marion Mountain Campground, it's difficult to locate the sites. This is because most of them are

CAMPGROUND RATINGS

Beauty: ★★★
Site privacy: ★★★★★
Site spaciousness: ★★★★★
Quiet: ★★★★★
Security: ★★★★
Cleanliness/upkeep: ★★★★★

Marion Mountain, nestled in the clouds, is a great break from nearby Los Angeles. Come for fun hiking and stay for good tent camping.

isolated from each other among the pines. The pitches, on pine needles, are nice and spongy. Through the pine boughs, you'll see the steep slopes of the mountains across the canyon, all covered with pines, oaks, and rocky tors.

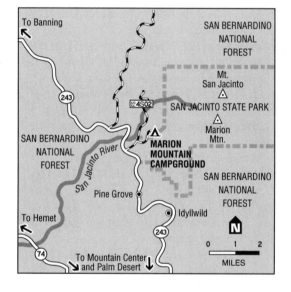

I brought along a portable radio/cassette player with a few classical music tapes. What a wonderful experience! Camping in the mountains goes with classical music. A music professor once told me that music began when primitive man, imbued with the "like produces like" principle, endeavored to wake the sleeping earth from its winter nap by beating it with a stick in the spring. From this came the percussion drums and then the more sophisticated woodwinds that imitated the birds.

To hike from the campground, go to site #12. Across from that site's picnic table, there is a dirt road that heads up the slope. Follow it for 20 yards and notice the trail arrows pointing right and left. The right arrows lead you down the hill to the trailhead. The left ones indicate the Marion Mountain Trail, which goes up into the State Park and joins the Pacific Crest Trail (PCT) near Deer Spring. It climbs the heavily forested northwest flank of Marion Mountain and is the shortest way to climb San Jacinto Peak.

Take plenty of water and be aware of thunderstorms. When there is lightning, avoid open areas like meadows, ridges, and mountaintops. Stay away from isolated trees and take cover under dense, small trees in lower areas, in a boulder field, or in a cave. Failing all this, lie flat on the ground. And, in all cases, remove metal frame backpacks and metal tent poles. Really, lightning is no joke. I suffered a near miss in the Mojave Desert a few summers ago. It burned my calves and scared me half to death.

In early September, when I last visited Marion Mountain, there were thunderstorm clouds over the mountains. The dry air carried a hint of rain. As we were hiking up the slopes around the campground, there was a roll of thunder, and a splatter of rain hit the dusty rocks. What drama! The campground host told me they'd had a hard storm hit in the middle of August. It rained like hell for a couple of hours, and then the sun came out. This is typical of the Southern Sierras in late August and September and something to watch for.

A good place for a sundowner is up the dirt road across from site #12. Go past the arrows for the Marion Mountain Trail. About 20 yards up, climb the ridge to the right, and there are some nice big boulders to sit on and watch the sun set. Back on the dirt road, walk to the end of it. There's a short trail that switchbacks up the slope to some cabins, where there is an incredible view of the southwest side of the range.

Head south to Pine Cove to find gas and ice. For a town with everything, go a few miles farther to Idyllwild, a lovely little mountain town. Idyllwild even has a shopping center with a supermarket and a hardware store. They have butchers, restaurants, artists, writers, and, of course, the San Jacinto Ranger Station—the left as you enter town. If Marion Mountain and the other campgrounds nearby are full, and/or you want to disperse camp or yellow-post camp, that's where you need to go. The rangers will fix you up with a fire permit and show you where to go.

KEY INFORMATION

Marion Mountain Campground, San Bernardino National Forest
San Jacinto Ranger District
P.O. Box 518, 54270 Pinecrest
Idyllwild, CA 92549

Operated by: U.S. Forest Service

Information: (909) 659-2117; www.r5.fs.fed.us/ sanbernardino

Open: May to mid-October

Individual sites: 24

Each site has: Picnic table, fire pit

Registration: At entrance; reserve by phone, (877) 444-6777, or online, www.reserveusa.com

Facilities: Water, pit toilets

Parking: Near site

Fee: $10, $5 for extra vehicle; $8.65 nonrefundable reservation fee

Elevation: 6,400 feet

Restrictions:

Pets—On leash only

Fires—In fire pit

Vehicles—No RVs longer than 15 feet

Other—No dogs allowed within Mt. San Jacinto State Park wilderness; permits are required to enter wilderness

To get there: from L.A., drive east to Banning. Go south on CA 243 for 22 miles. Turn left at FS 4S02 and drive 1.7 miles to the campground.

PASO PICACHO CAMPGROUND

Cuyamaca Rancho State Park

This campground will keep you coming back season after season. Even in the dead of winter, under a blanket of snow, the days have a warm promise about them, which is reflected in the wonderful patchwork of pines, oak, and open meadows. The atmosphere is drowsy. Even the apple trees seem to find it easygoing.

The rain and their geographical location, between coast and desert, make the Cuyamacas a unique ecosystem. I spent a year working on a private nature preserve on North Peak and never saw a day in Cuyamaca that didn't have some calm majesty. Even the rattlesnakes are forgiving. I've stepped on several of them, and they just eyed me with mild rebuke and slithered away.

Although it's true there was a recent mountain lion attack on a jogger here, I maintain it was a pilot error. Mountain lions have notoriously bad eyesight and make regrettable misjudgments. If I'm ever lucky enough to see one (the Native Americans called them ghosts), I shall stand dead still, then rise up and try to look like a grizzly bear.

Paso Picacho means "mountain pass," and *Cuyamaca* in Native American means "rain above." Most of Cuyamaca State Park was in the Cuyamaca Rancho, about 35,501 acres of meadow and mountain timberland granted to Agustin Olvera by Governor Pio Pico in 1845. There's no

CAMPGROUND RATINGS

Beauty: ★★★★
Site privacy: ★★★
Site spaciousness: ★★★★
Quiet: ★★★
Security: ★★★★★
Cleanliness/upkeep: ★★★★

Paso Picacho Campground, blessed with meadows and mountains, is good for any time of year. Reserve ahead for peak times.

record of how the resident Native Americans felt about it—unless random acts of mayhem and vandalism are translated as disapproval. Olvera didn't care much for his Rancho and sold it in 1869, just before William Skidmore chased his stray mule around Cuyamaca Lake and spotted gold not far from the present Paso Picacho Campground. Skidmore filed a claim and opened a mine calling it Stonewall Jackson after the Civil War General. Local GAR (Grand Army of the

Republic) veterans protested, and the mine became Stonewall Mine, befitting the rocky mountain behind it. Before the mine closed in 1893, more than $2 million worth of gold was taken from it ($2 million in 1893 dollars).

Most of the Rancho was sold to the state for the park. The lake is leased to the Cuyamaca Recreation and Park District. The ore cars and other relics from the old Stonewall Mine were rolled down the mine's open, 630-foot shaft. The buildings were sold for scrap to a Los Angeles wrecking company.

The Paso Picacho Campground is roomy and well planned with flat, drained tent sites and clean rest rooms featuring flush toilets and showers. It is clean and well patrolled. It feels like a campground from the 1950s. The campers who come to Paso Picacho tend to be hikers, fishing people, or bird watchers (almost 300 species of birds have been observed in the park) who tend to come back year after year. They appreciate the four seasons of Cuyamaca and the more than 100 miles of hiking and equestrian trails.

Don't forget nearby Julian, which has blossomed into a relentlessly pleasing tourist attraction in the last 25 years. But don't come if you don't like apple pie. The cafe on Cuyamaca Lake with its very friendly staff and sunny outside deck is perfect for breakfast, lunch, or an afternoon beer. Wally's Waterwagon across the road and down a little is perfect for a less sedate happy hour or country western band later on. Climb the 3.5-mile Cuyamaca Peak Trail from the campground to the summit for a spectacular view of the Pacific Ocean, the desert, Mexico, and the distant Salton Sea.

Watch for raptors (birds of prey). You might see golden eagles, red-shouldered hawks, bald eagles, and turkey vultures. Think like a mouse; you'll find raptors where their prey is located. Fields with good perches nearby are excellent places to see raptors.

KEY INFORMATION

Paso Picacho Campground
Cuyamaca Rancho State Park
12511 Highway 79
Descanso, CA 91916

Operated by: California Department of Parks and Recreation

Information: (760) 765-0755 or (760) 765-3023; http://parks.ca.gov.

Open: All year

Individual sites: 83

Each site has: Picnic table, fire ring

Registration: By entrance; reserve by phone, (800) 444-7275, or online, www.reserveamerica.com

Facilities: Water, flush toilets, showers, wood for sale

Parking: At individual site

Fee: $12; $8.65 nonrefundable reservation fee

Elevation: 4,900 feet

Restrictions:
Pets—On leash only
Fires—In fireplace
Vehicles—RVs up to 27 feet and trailers up to 24 feet allowed
Other—Reservations on holidays and summer weekends recommended

To get there: from L.A., take I-10 east to I-15. Go south to Temecula. Take CA 79 southeast 11 miles past Julian to the campground entrance on the right.

WILLIAM HEISE COUNTY PARK

Julian

A mong the many reasons to tent camp in William Heise County Park are the incredible drives in from L.A. via Warner Springs or from San Diego via Ramona or Cuyamaca Rancho State Park. All three show Southern California at its most charming and very best—the rolling, forested hills, the green meadows, the tiny western towns. This was the real gold the forty-niners found when they arrived in California—this beautiful land. On all three drives, near Julian, you climb 2 miles south on Pine Hills Road, then left on Frisius Drive. Those final 2 miles carry you through farmland that echoes of bucolic Vermont or New Hampshire. The resemblance is eerie. You can only imagine the argonauts; after walking 3,000 miles across the continent they must have looked around Frisius Drive and thought, "My God! I'm home."

The 900 acres of oak, pine, and cedar, William Heise County Park are Upper Chaparral; this area is also known as Cold Chaparral because most of the precipitation comes from snow and fog drip. As you hike around and in the park, watch the slope orientation to see the effect. On south-facing slopes there are evergreen shrubs with thick oval leaves like the manzanita. Note how the manzanita leaves are mealy and waxy and are often oriented vertically to reduce the amount of light that directly strikes the leaf surface.

CAMPGROUND RATINGS

Beauty: ★★★★
Site privacy: ★★
Site spaciousness: ★★★
Quiet: ★★★
Security: ★★★
Cleanliness/upkeep: ★★★

Visit California high country and feel like you're in Vermont all at once. This campground near historic Julian offers solid enjoyment.

Manzanita endure droughts, resist fire, and withstand cold. On north-facing slopes look for California live oak; Jeffrey, Coulter, sugar, and poderosa pines; white fir; and incense cedar.

Like Cuyamaca Rancho State Park, William Heise is birder's paradise. Look for various hawks, eagles, owls, woodpeckers, vireos, warblers, sparrows, and the like. Also, look for the full complement of Southern California reptiles and various rodents eating the plethora of acorns. Acorns were a

Cahuilla Native American staple, made into a meal and then bread.

Once, camping at William Heise, we experimented with acorn bread. First, we ground the acorns into a coarse meal, then following local Cahuilla recipe, we filled a colander with fine sand, patted the coarsely ground acorn meal down into a bowl-like depression in the sand, and poured water slowly over the meal to leach out the bitterness. Then we pounded the meal down finer in a mortar until it resembled a fine powder. Finally, the meal was sifted, mixed with water, and baked on a hot rock—not bad, but a little bitter.

Encouraged, my camping companion resolved to fatten up a pig on the acorns in his yard at home. He found a candidate piglet and penned it up under his oak trees. For weeks, it ate acorns heartily. Then, a carelessly guarded plate of chicken enchiladas and refried beans was left out. The pig got it, and that was it; his palate was ruined. No more acorns. He rejected Native American cuisine, and finally became Thanksgiving dinner himself.

Heise is a friendly place to camp. Half of the sites are for tents only, which separates you from the RVs that feel like city blocks on wheels when you're lying there in a little tent. The park is roomy, and the rest rooms are very clean. Once, we rented one of the two rental cabins at Heise. It had six wooden bunks and a maximum capacity of eight ($35 per night plus reservation fee). Bring your own bedding and a padlock for the door. Cooking is done outside on a barbecue. It was as jolly as a good school trip. For reservations, call (858) 565-3600.

Heise is a fine base camp from which to explore Julian, Wynola, and Santa Ysabel. Do an apple pie comparison test. Stop for a drink or breakfast at the much-fabled Pine Hills Lodge by the junction of Pine Hills Road and Frisius Drive. Visit the Santa Ysabel Mission 2 miles north of Santa Ysabel on CA 79. See the museum in Julian. Take the Eagle Mine tour. Ask the ranger/campground host at Heise about trips to Boulder Creek and Boulder Creek Falls. Don't miss a killer hike (11 miles round-trip) down Kelly Ditch Trail to Cuyamaca Rancho State Park.

To get there: from L.A., take I-10 east to I-15. Go south to Temecula. Take CA 79 southeast to Santa Ysabel. Go left toward Julian 5.8 miles to Pine Hills Road. Go right and drive 2 miles to Frisius Drive and make a left. Go 2 miles, and you are at the park.

KEY INFORMATION

William Heise County Park Department of Parks and Recreation
5201 Ruffin Road, Suite P
San Diego, CA 92123-1699

Operated by: San Diego County Department of Parks and Recreation

Information: (858) 694-3049; www.co.san-diego.ca.us/cnty/cntydepts/landuse/parks/camping

Open: Weekend of Palm Sunday until week after Thanksgiving

Individual sites: 43 tents only; 40 tents or RVs

Each site has: Picnic table, fire ring, tent pad, water nearby

Registration: By entrance; for reservations call (858) 565-3600

Facilities: Water, flush toilets, showers, playground

Parking: At individual site

Fee: $12 for tent, $14 for RV, $3 reservation fee per site

Elevation: 4,200 feet

Restrictions:

Pets—On leash only; $1 fee; not allowed on hiking trails

Fires—In fire ring

Vehicles—Motor homes, small trailers

Other—No generators; checkout time is 2 P.M.; day use parking is $2 per vehicle

APPENDICES

APPENDIX A
Camping Equipment Checklist

Except for the large and bulky items on this list, I keep a plastic storage container full of the essentials of car camping so that they're ready to go when I am. I make a last-minute check of the inventory, resupply anything that's low or missing, and away I go!

Cooking Utensils
Bottle opener
Bottles of salt, pepper, spices, sugar, cooking oil, and maple syrup in waterproof, spill-proof containers
Can opener
Corkscrew
Cups, plastic or tin
Dish soap (biodegradable), sponge, and towel
Flatware
Food of your choice
Frying pan
Fuel for stove
Matches in waterproof container
Plates
Pocketknife
Pot with lid
Spatula
Stove
Tin foil
Wooden spoon

First Aid Kit
Band-Aids
First aid cream
Gauze pads
Ibuprofen or aspirin
Insect repellent
Moleskin
Snakebite kit (if you're heading for desert conditions)
Sunscreen/chapstick
Tape, waterproof adhesive

Sleeping Gear
Pillow
Sleeping bag
Sleeping pad, inflatable or insulated
Tent with ground tarp and rainfly

Miscellaneous
Bath soap (biodegradable), washcloth, and towel
Camp chair
Candles
Cooler
Deck of cards
Fire starter
Flashlight with fresh batteries
Foul weather clothing (useful year-round in the Northwest)
Paper towels
Plastic zip-top bags
Sunglasses
Toilet paper
Water bottle
Wool blanket

Optional
Barbecue grill
Binoculars
Books on bird, plant, and wildlife identification
Fishing rod and tackle
Hatchet
Lantern
Maps (road, topographic, trails, etc.)

APPENDIX B
Suggested Reading

The Anza-Borrego Desert Region. Lindsay, Lowell and Diana. Wilderness Press, 1991.

Best Short Hikes in California's Northern Sierra. Whitehill, Karen and Terry. The Mountaineers, 1990.

Best Short Hikes in California's Southern Sierra. Whitehill, Karen and Terry. The Mountaineers, 1991.

California Camping. Stienstra, Tom. Foghorn Press, 1994.

California's Desert Trails. Chase, J. Smeaton. Tioga Publishing Co., 1987.

California's Eastern Sierra. Irwin, Sue. Cachuma Press, 1991.

Day Hiking Kings Canyon. Sorensen, Steve. Manzanita Press, 1992.

Day Hiking Sequoia. Sorensen, Steve. Manzanita Press, 1992.

Exploring the Southern Sierra: East Side. Jenkins, J.C. and Ruby Johnson. Jenkins and Jenkins, 1995.

Exploring the Southern Sierra: West Side. Jenkins, J.C. and Ruby Johnson. Jenkins and Jenkins, 1992.

Gem Trails of California. Mitchel, James R. Gem Guides Book Co., 1986.

Gold! Gold! Petralia, Joseph F. Sierra Outdoor Products Co., 1992.

A Natural History of California. Schoenherr, Allan A. University of California Press, 1992.

Roadside Plants of Southern California. Belzer, Thomas J. Mountain Press, 1984.

San Bernardino Mountain Trails. Robinson, John W. Wilderness Press, 1986.

A Treasury of the Sierra Nevada. Reid, Robert Leonard. Wilderness Press, 1983.

Walking California's State Parks. McKinney, John. HarperCollins West, 1994.

Walking Southern California. McKinney, John. HarperCollins West, 1992.

APPENDIX C
Sources of Information

B.L.M., California State Office
2800 Cottage Way, Suite W1834
Sacramento, CA 95825-1886
(916) 978-4400f
www.blm.ca.gov

California Parks and Recreation
P.O. Box 942896
Sacramento, CA 94296
(916) 653-6995
www.parks.ca.gov

Death Valley National Park
P.O. Box 579
Death Valley, CA 92328
(760) 786-2331
www.nps.gov/deva

Inyo National Forest
873 N. Main St.,
Bishop, CA 93514
(760) 873-2400
www.r5.fs.fed.us/inyo

Joshua Tree National Park
74485 National Park Drive
Twentynine Palms, CA 92277-3597
(760) 367-5500
www.nps.gov/jotr

Los Padres National Forest
6755 Hollister Ave., Suite 150
Goleta, CA 93117
(805) 968-6640
www.r5.fs.fed.us/lospadres

Mojave National Preserve
222 E. Main St., Suite 202
Barstow, CA 92311
(760) 255-8800
www.nps.gov/moja

N.P.S., Pacific West Region
600 Harrison Street, Suite 600
San Francisco, CA 94107
(415) 244-2978
www.nps.gov

San Bernidino National Forest
1824 Commercenter Circle
San Bernardino, CA 92408-3430
(909) 884-6634
www.r5.fs.fed.us/sanbernadino

Sequoia/Kings Canyon National Park
47050 Generals Highway
Three Rivers, CA 93271-9651
(559) 565-3341
www.nps.gov/seki

Sequoia National Forest
900 West Grand Avenue
Porterville, CA 93257
(559) 784-1500
www.r5.fs.fed.us/sequoia

Sierra National Forest
1600 Tollhouse Road
Clovis, CA 93612
(559) 297-0706
www.r5.fs.fed.us/sierra

Yosemite National Park
PO Box 577
Yosemite National Park, CA 95389
(209) 372-0200
www.nps.gov/yose

U.S.F.S., Pacific Southwest Region
1323 Club Drive
Vallejo, CA 94592
(707)562.8737
www.r5.fs.fed.us

INDEX

ABOUT THE AUTHOR

Working for the Denver Museum of Natural History, Bill's mother was an avid camper, and she developed in her son a love for the outdoors. Inspired by the Native American "digs" that his mother worked on and their many camping jaunts to Maine, the Adirondacks, and numerous locations in the West, Bill continued to foster his enthusiasm for camping.

Driven by his sense of adventure, Bill did a stint in Pernambuco, Brazil, after college, working for the Peace Corps on a small rancher's cooperative. Reminiscent of 1830s New Mexico, there were no cars and no electricity, but an abundance of cattle drives and gunfights in the streets.

After shaking off the chaps and spurs, Bill donned the vestments of academia to teach at several colleges around London. In the interim, he composed several short stories and a novel. Unwilling to give up his roots, he continued to camp in England, biking down old county lanes and camping in farming fields overnight.

Now Bill lives in Santa Monica, California, where he continues to write screenplays and wonderful books about his love of camping, including *The Best in Tent Camping: Southern California*, the series counterpart to this book. And of course, he continues to travel extensively on camping and fishing expeditions around Baja California and California proper.